I0416900

July 2013

NAVY SHIPBUILDING

Significant Investments in the Littoral Combat Ship Continue Amid Substantial Unknowns about Capabilities, Use, and Cost

GAO-13-530

G A O

Accountability * Integrity * Reliability

Highlights

Highlights of GAO-13-530, a report to congressional requesters

NAVY SHIPBUILDING
Significant Investments in the Littoral Combat Ship Continue Amid Substantial Unknowns about Capabilities, Use, and Cost

Why GAO Did This Study

The Navy's LCS consists of the ship—called a seaframe—and mission packages, which provide combat capability. LCS is intended to be reconfigurable to perform three primary missions: surface warfare; mine countermeasures; and anti-submarine warfare. The Navy currently plans to buy 52 seaframes, including two variants being constructed at two U.S. shipyards, and 64 mission packages. The total estimated acquisition cost is about $40 billion in 2010 dollars.

GAO was asked to assess the status of the LCS program. This report examines (1) the progress and challenges associated with seaframe and mission module production, development, and testing; and (2) the soundness of the Navy's business case for the integrated LCS program. GAO analyzed Navy and contractor documents, toured shipyards and LCS ships, and interviewed DOD and Navy officials and contractor representatives.

What GAO Recommends

To ensure that LCS investments are informed by key information, Congress should consider restricting funding for further ships until the Navy completes several studies about future LCS designs and capabilities. GAO is also making several recommendations, including that DOD limit future seaframe and mission package purchases until it achieves key acquisition and testing milestones. DOD disagreed with these recommendations, stating that slowing seaframe purchases would cause prices to rise and mission package purchases are needed to equip operational ships. GAO believes the Navy does not have adequate knowledge about LCS capabilities to support the planned procurement rate.

View GAO-13-530. For more information, contact Michele Mackin at (202) 512-4841 or mackinm@gao.gov.

What GAO Found

The Littoral Combat Ship (LCS) seaframe program continues to face challenges stemming from concurrent design, production, and testing activities. The Navy has taken steps to resolve problems with the lead ships, and the shipyards are beginning to realize benefits from facility improvements and experience. However, testing remains to be completed and the Navy is currently studying potentially significant design changes, such as increasing the commonality of systems between the two ship variants and changing ship capabilities. Changes at this point can compromise the positive impacts of shipyard learning, increase costs, and prolong schedules. The mission module program also has concurrency issues, and testing to date has shown considerable limitations in capabilities. The Navy is pursuing an incremental approach to fielding mission packages, but it has yet to finalize the requirements for each increment and does not plan to achieve the minimum performance requirements for the mine countermeasures and surface warfare packages until the final increments are fielded in 2017 and 2019, respectively.

The Navy continues to buy LCS seaframes and modules even as significant questions remain about the program and its underlying business case. Elements of the LCS business case, including its cost, the time needed to develop and field the system, and its anticipated capabilities have degraded over time. There are also significant unknowns related to key LCS operations and support concepts and the relative advantages and disadvantages of the two seaframe variants. The potential effect of these unknowns on the program is compounded by the Navy's aggressive acquisition strategy. By the time key tests of integrated LCS capability are completed in several years, the Navy will have procured or have under contract more than half of the planned number of seaframes. Almost half of the planned seaframes are already under contract, and the Navy plans to award further contracts in 2016, before the Department of Defense (DOD) makes a decision about full rate production of the ships. The Navy will not be able to demonstrate that mission packages integrated with the seaframes can meet the minimum performance requirements until operational testing for both variants (*Freedom and Independence*) is completed, currently planned for 2019.

Alignment of Planned Littoral Combat Ship Seaframe Contract and Test Activities

Cumulative seaframe purchases (includes both funded and planned)

		Solicit proposals and source selection		Contract award		Full rate production decision	
12	**16**	**20**	**24**	**26**	**28**	**30**	**33**
FY 2012	FY 2013	FY 2014	FY 2015	FY 2016	FY 2017	FY 2018	FY 2019

Freedom variant operational testing

Independence variant operational testing

Source: GAO analysis of Navy data.

The Navy has also essentially bypassed two major acquisition reviews for mission modules, purchasing 8 of the 64 planned mission packages before gaining approval to enter the system development and initial production phases.

_____ **United States Government Accountability Office**

Contents

Figures

Abbreviations

ASW	Anti-Submarine Warfare
CONOPS	Concept of Operations
DOD	Department of Defense
DOT&E	Director, Operational Test and Evaluation
INSURV	Board of Inspection and Survey
LCS	Littoral Combat Ship
MCM	Mine Countermeasures
PSA	Post Shakedown Availability
OPNAV	Office of the Chief of Naval Operations
RMMV	Remote Multi-Mission Vehicle
SUW	Surface Warfare
USD (AT&L)	Undersecretary of Defense for Acquisition, Technology and Logistics

GAO

U.S. GOVERNMENT ACCOUNTABILITY OFFICE

441 G St. N.W.
Washington, DC 20548

July 22, 2013

The Honorable Carl Levin
Chairman
Committee on Armed Services
United States Senate

The Honorable John McCain
Ranking Member
Subcommittee on Seapower
Committee on Armed Services
United States Senate

The Honorable J. Randy Forbes
Chairman
The Honorable Mike McIntyre
Ranking Member
Subcommittee on Seapower and Projection Forces
Committee on Armed Services
House of Representatives

The Navy's Littoral Combat Ship (LCS) is intended to be reconfigurable to perform three different primary missions: mine countermeasures (MCM), surface warfare (SUW), and anti-submarine warfare (ASW). The LCS consists of two distinct parts—the ship itself (called a seaframe because of its ability to carry interchangeable payloads similarly to an airframe) and the interchangeable package of sensors and weapons that it carries and deploys, called a mission package. The mission package provides the majority of the ship's combat capability. Mission packages are composed of one or more mission modules and an aviation capability. The Navy has contracted for 24 seaframes, consisting of two design variants being constructed at two U.S. shipyards. The Navy has also procured 8 mission packages, with plans to procure 2 more in 2013. In its baselines, the Navy planned to spend over $40 billion in 2010 dollars through fiscal year 2034 to acquire 55 LCS seaframes and 64 mission packages—though it has since reduced the total number of seaframes to 52.

The Navy has accepted delivery of the first three seaframes, and has spent several years completing various test and maintenance events on the first two—USS *Freedom* (LCS 1) and USS *Independence* (LCS 2); USS *Fort Worth* (LCS 3) was delivered in June 2012. During this time, we and others have identified a number of problems with the seaframes and their equipment, as well as challenges related to the development of mission module technologies. In light of these issues, you asked us to conduct a broad evaluation of the LCS program. This report addresses the following: (1) the Navy's progress in producing and testing LCS seaframes and any remaining risks; (2) the Navy's progress in developing, producing, and testing LCS mission modules and any remaining risks; (3) any risks in the Navy's acquisition strategy for the integrated LCS program.

To conduct our work, we evaluated the Navy's acquisition strategies; requirements documentation; concepts of operations; test and delivery schedules; test plans; and life-cycle cost estimates for the two seaframe variants and the mission modules. In addition, we interviewed the Under Secretary of Defense for Acquisition, Technology and Logistics; the Director, Operational Test and Evaluation; Deputy Directors for Cost Assessment and Program Evaluation; the Director of Navy Staff; officials from the Office of the Chief of Naval Operations (OPNAV, who represent the sponsors of the LCS program); LCS program office officials; and officials from Fleet Forces Command, LCS Squadron One, and the Third, Fourth, Fifth, and Seventh Fleets; among others. We analyzed Navy and contractor documentation on the seaframes and mission modules programs related to development, production, testing, performance, and fielding. We discussed this information with government and contractor representatives responsible for managing these programs and testing key LCS mission systems. We also visited both shipyards and toured the three LCS ships that have been delivered to the Navy to date. A more detailed description of our scope and methodology is presented in appendix I.

We conducted this performance audit from April 2012 to July 2013 in accordance with generally accepted government auditing standards. Those standards require that we plan and perform the audit to obtain sufficient, appropriate evidence to provide a reasonable basis for our findings and conclusions based on our audit objectives. We believe that the evidence obtained provides a reasonable basis for our findings and conclusions based on our audit objectives.

Background

The concept for the LCS emerged in the late 1990s and early 2000s as the Navy was trying to address two main needs. First, it had identified existing and emerging capability gaps in its ability to defeat large numbers of hostile small boats, sea mines, and quiet diesel-electric and nuclear-powered submarines, especially when these threats were present in the shallow waters close to shore, which are known as the littorals. Second, the Navy wanted to field an affordable utility ship that would be able to handle some of the day-to-day tasks and responsibilities of the Navy, including missions such as counter-piracy patrols and foreign nation training exercises that are relatively low risk. As the number of frigates has declined over time, these missions are increasingly being performed by more expensive and capable ships—destroyers and cruisers—which the Navy states are in high demand for more stressing operations. In addition, an affordable ship class was needed if the Navy hoped to maintain its fleet size while dealing with a tightening shipbuilding budget for new surface combatants.

To fulfill these goals, the Navy settled on a set of novel concepts that would be realized on a new class of ships—LCS. LCS would have interchangeable mission systems in the form of mission modules rather than fixed mission systems as is generally the case with other Navy surface combatants. These modules would give the Navy flexibility to change equipment in the field to meet different mission needs, and to incorporate new technology to address emerging threats. LCS was also envisioned as having a greatly reduced crew size compared to other ship classes, which in turn would lead to lower costs for operations and support. To balance these reduced manning levels with its operational, maintenance, support, and administrative needs, the Navy developed a new maintenance and support concept. Unlike other ships, LCS would have no onboard administrative personnel and a limited ability to conduct maintenance at sea; instead, it would rely heavily on shore-based support. The Navy also opted to use a rotational crewing concept, whereby multiple crews are assigned to one ship and rotate on and off while the ship remains forward deployed. Rotational crewing is used on the ballistic missile submarines, mine countermeasures ships, and coastal patrol craft, but it is not widely used on U.S. Navy surface combatants.

The Navy formally initiated the LCS acquisition program in 2004. At that time, the LCS seaframe and mission modules acquisition efforts were managed as one program. In 2011, the Navy requested that they be separated into two programs managed by two distinct program offices, which would fall under a newly formed Program Executive Office. The LCS seaframe program office is responsible for the hull; various command and control systems; core combat systems such as radars and the 57-millimeter gun; and launch, handling, and recovery systems that deploy mission module equipment. The mission modules program office is responsible for buying and integrating the systems that come together to form the three different mission packages—MCM, ASW, and SUW.

The Navy is procuring two different seaframe designs from shipbuilding teams led by Lockheed Martin—which builds its ships at Marinette Marine in Marinette, Wisconsin—and Austal USA in Mobile, Alabama.[1] The two designs reflect different contractor solutions to the same set of performance requirements. The most notable difference is that the Lockheed Martin *Freedom* variant (LCS 1 and other odd-numbered seaframes, 3 through 23) is a monohull design with a steel hull and aluminum superstructure, while the Austal USA *Independence* variant (LCS 2 and other even-numbered seaframes, 4 through 24) is an aluminum trimaran.[2] This report refers to the Lockheed Martin ships as the *Freedom* variant and the Austal USA ships as the *Independence* variant.

Figure 1 shows the first two LCS seaframes.

---

[1]For LCS 2 and LCS 4, General Dynamics was the prime contractor for the Austal USA-built ships. General Dynamics and Austal USA ended their teaming arrangement in 2010. Austal USA is the prime contractor for the 10 other even-numbered seaframes currently under contract.

[2]A trimaran is a ship that has three separate hulls. The Navy is now referring to the *Independence*-class variant as a slender stabilized monohull design.

Figure 1: Littoral Combat Ship (LCS) Seaframe Variants

Source: Lockheed Martin (image).

Freedom variant

Source: General Dynamics (image).

Independence variant

Each seaframe has reconfigurable spaces where the mission modules are carried. These spaces are equipped with standardized connections for ship services including power and cooling. The mission module designs are based on standard shipping containers that are outfitted with a variety of unmanned systems, sensors, and weapons that can be loaded onto and off of the seaframe. Mission modules are also accompanied by an aviation detachment, consisting of a helicopter and its flight and support crew, as well as vertical take-off unmanned aerial vehicles. When the aviation detachment is embarked with a mission module and the mission module crew, it is referred to as a mission package. The Navy is fielding the mission packages in increments in order to deliver capabilities faster. The Navy plans on fielding one ASW increment and four MCM and SUW increments. The Navy will upgrade all mission packages to the same configuration once the final increment of each has been fielded. The Navy plans to buy 64 mission packages: 16 ASW packages, 24 MCM packages, and 24 SUW packages.

The Navy's acquisition strategy for LCS seaframes has changed several times over the past decade. The original plan was to fund one or two initial ships—in what the Navy called a Flight 0 configuration—based on the designs it selected through a conceptual design competition, and then spend time experimenting with the seaframes and overall LCS concept. This experimentation time was considered important to help inform what the Navy wanted and needed in the seaframe, and also to help determine if the LCS concept was feasible. Further, although both designs met the Navy's requirements, their significant differences lent even more importance to the experimentation concept to inform a decision about which seaframe design was better suited to meet the Navy's needs. After a down-select decision, the winning design was to be procured in larger numbers, with any design changes incorporated into a new Flight 1 configuration. The Navy abandoned this strategy, however, after concluding it would be unrealistic to expect the two competing shipyards to build only one or two ships and then wait for the Navy to complete the period of experimentation before awarding additional contracts. Instead, the Navy opted to continue funding additional seaframes. This decision meant that the Navy would buy a number of seaframes without having completed the planned period of discovery and learning. The Navy has made several other revisions to the LCS acquisition strategy over time, including shifting back and forth between plans to down-select to one seaframe design or to build both. Table 1 shows the evolution of the Navy's LCS acquisition strategy, and relevant contracting actions.

Table 1: Major Changes in Navy's Littoral Combat Ship (LCS) Acquisition and Contracting Strategy

Date	Acquisition strategy action	Contracting action	Description
Early concept— approx. 2000-2004	●		Two shipyards would each build one Flight 0 prototype. These prototypes would be tested by experimentation in the fleet, which would inform design changes or a decision to down-select; that is, to buy only one variant.
December 2004 and October 2005		●	Navy awards cost-reimbursable contracts for detailed design and construction for LCS 1 and LCS 2, respectively. The Navy paid for these ships with research and development funds.
2005	●		The Navy decides to continue procurement of both Flight 0 seaframe designs at least through fiscal year 2009. Experimentation will now occur concurrently with buying seaframes.
June and December 2006[a]		●	Navy exercises contract options for construction of the LCS 3 and LCS 4, respectively.
April and November 2007		●	After unsuccessful negotiations to change the contracts for LCS 3 and 4 from cost-reimbursable type to fixed price incentive contracts to manage excessive cost growth, the Navy terminates these contracts in part.
September 2008	●		Navy decides to continue buying both variants with no plans to down-select to a single ship design, and to incorporate design changes and lessons learned into what it terms a Flight 0+ configuration.
March and May 2009		●	Navy awards fixed price contracts to both shipyards for LCS 3 and 4.
January 2010	●		Navy approves plans for a down-select in fiscal year 2010 to a single design to be procured in a block buy of up to ten ships over 5 years. This strategy is intended to obtain more competitive pricing. The Navy plans for two ships in fiscal year 2010 and two more ships per year from fiscal years 2011-2014. The Navy strategy also included a requirement to bring in a second shipbuilder to build five ships of the winning design.

Date	Acquisition strategy action	Contracting action	Description
November 2010	●		As a result of receiving competitive pricing from both the shipbuilders during negotiations, the Navy decides to continue buying both designs and award a ten-ship block buy contract to each contractor. Navy requests and obtains congressional approval for this change.
December 2010		●	Navy awards two block buy contracts for up to ten ships to both shipyards; the Navy authorizes construction of one ship at each shipyard at the time of contract award, and plans to authorize construction of one ship at each shipyard in fiscal year 2011, and two ships at each shipyard per year, from fiscal years 2012-2015.

Source: GAO analysis of Navy LCS acquisition strategies.

[a]From 2006-2008, 5 seaframes, including the original LCS 3 and LCS 4 which the Navy contracted for in June and December of 2006, respectively, were canceled by the Navy as a result of program restructuring or congressional action. The actions cancelling 3 of these seaframes are not included above because they occurred prior to a contract being awarded.

As indicated by table 2 below, the Navy has contracted for 24 LCS seaframes to date. Under the block buy contracts it negotiated with the two shipbuilders in November 2010, the Navy negotiated prices upfront for the seaframes. However, the shipyards cannot proceed with work in connection with the ships until the Navy provides written notice that funds are available and have been obligated to the contract.

Table 2: Status of Littoral Combat Ship (LCS) Seaframes

Seaframe number	Status as of March 2013
1-3	Navy has accepted delivery
4-10	Under construction at the two shipyards
11-16	Under contract with the two shipyards; congressional funding has been received
17-24	Under contract but not yet congressionally funded

Source: Navy documentation.

The Navy requested funding for LCS 17-20 in its fiscal year 2014 budget request and plans to request funding for LCS 21-24 in its fiscal year 2015 request. In any given fiscal year, if funds are not available to fully fund the ships planned for that year, the shipyards can renegotiate the prices and delivery schedules for those ships and any additional ships covered by the block buy contracts that have not yet started construction.[3] However, the target prices for the seaframes already funded and under construction would not be affected and any remaining unfunded ships are not to be considered terminated for the convenience of the government. According to the Navy, the cost of the funded ships might still increase under this scenario because of increases in the overhead costs applied to those ships. The Navy and shipbuilders would share some of these costs and the shipbuilders may have to absorb the remainder of these costs if the increases cause the total seaframe construction cost to exceed the ceiling price in the contract.[4] The Navy expects to take delivery of the last seaframes under these contracts in 2019. In 2013, the Navy announced it was reducing the number of planned seaframe purchases from 55 to 52, based on changing force structure requirements.

In 2012, two independent Navy studies—one conducted by the Board of Inspection and Survey (INSURV, the Navy's ship inspection entity) and one conducted by the office of the Chief of Naval Operations—identified concerns with the LCS and recommended steps to improve aspects of the program.[5] Partially in response, in August 2012, the Chief of Naval Operations established an LCS oversight council. The council is composed of vice admirals from the requirements, acquisition, and fleet communities, and has the mission of ensuring "the successful procurement, development, manning, training, sustainment, and operational employment" of the LCS, mission packages, and shore

---

[3]In the situation that funds are not available in any given fiscal year for the ships planned for that year, and the parties renegotiate the prices and delivery schedules for those ships and any additional ships covered by the block buy contracts that have not yet started construction, it does not constitute a termination for the convenience of the government and, thus, the government would not pay termination costs.

[4]The LCS block buy contracts include fixed-price incentive line items for seaframe construction. Fixed-price incentive contracts include a target cost and a target profit, which together equal the target price. The block buy contracts also specify an incentive ratio for sharing any savings in the event of underruns when the actual contract cost is less than the target cost, or the sharing of additional costs when the actual contract cost is greater than this target cost. Under the LCS block buy contracts, the Navy's share of any cost savings or cost overrun is 50 percent and the shipbuilder's share is 50 percent. This cost sharing arrangement ends when the actual contract cost reaches the contract ceiling price, at which point the contractor is responsible for all additional costs. However, if the Navy is responsible for the cost overruns, it may be responsible for the costs associated with an increase in the contract ceiling price.

[5]Board of Inspection and Survey, *LCS Material Condition and Maintainability Report* (July 13, 2012) and Office of the Chief of Naval Operations *Review of the Navy's Readiness to Receive, Employ and Deploy the LCS Class Vessel*, (March 9, 2012).

infrastructure. The council's chairman carries the authority of the Chief of Naval Operations, and its first task was to develop a comprehensive plan to address the recommendations in the independent studies and concepts of operations (CONOPS) and doctrine issues needed to help support the planned April 2013 deployment of LCS 1 to Singapore. The first installment of the LCS Council's plan was issued in January 2013 and the plan currently contains over 1,000 action items. In March 2013, the Chief of Naval Operations added the Joint High Speed Vessel—also constructed at Austal USA—to the LCS Council's purview, citing the unique challenges facing both classes.[6]

One major activity identified in the LCS Council's plan is for both seaframe variants to complete testing to demonstrate their performance. DOD acquisition policy requires defense acquisition programs execute and complete developmental testing and operational testing. Developmental testing is intended to assist in identifying system performance, capabilities, limitations, and safety issues to help reduce design and programmatic risks. Operational testing is intended to assess a weapon system's capability in a realistic environment when maintained and operated by warfighters, subjected to routine wear-and-tear, and employed in combat conditions. Operational testing also includes live-fire testing, which provides timely assessment of the survivability and lethality of a weapon system. Survivability tests are another type of test, which demonstrate that the ship designs can safely absorb and control damage and includes a full ship shock trial, where a manned ship is subjected to a controlled, underwater explosion at sea. Statute requires a program to complete realistic survivability tests and initial operational testing before proceeding beyond low-rate initial production.[7]

Prior to acceptance, ships are also typically required to go through various trials to verify that requirements and specifications are met. An acceptance trial is first conducted by INSURV to determine whether the ship has been completed in accordance with the contract specifications and is operationally ready. After further Navy tests and evaluations, INSURV conducts a final contract trial to operationally demonstrate that the ship's systems satisfy material readiness conditions before the contract period ends and it is delivered to the fleet. Following acceptance and before initial deployment, the Navy also has the opportunity to make

---

[6]This change also adds the commander of the Military Sealift Command to the Council leadership. Military Sealift Command will operate the Joint High Speed Vessel.

[7]10 U.S.C. §§ 2399, 2366.

any needed additional corrections or to fix any problems that may have emerged in testing during a repair period called a post-shakedown availability (PSA). LCS 1 has completed her trials and PSA; LCS 2 has completed one PSA with a second one planned and has a remaining trial; LCS 3 has had both trials and is now entering a PSA period.

Seaframe Quality and Cost Should Continue to Improve, but Delays Persist and Potentially Significant Design Changes Could Disrupt Production Efficiency

The Navy has made progress in addressing some of the early design and construction problems on LCS 1 and LCS 2, and is obtaining better cost performance from the shipyards on follow-on seaframes now that the seaframes are in steady production. However, schedule delays persist. Based on projected shipyard learning curve improvements, shipyard performance can be expected to continue to improve over time. But, this expected progress may be disrupted because the Navy is considering new, potentially significant seaframe design changes that could disrupt production efficiency and learning. Neither variant has yet completed developmental testing to validate its performance or shock and survivability testing. Late discoveries in testing while seaframes continue to be constructed could lead to further design changes.

Navy Making Progress on Resolving Early Seaframe Quality Issues

The Navy has made progress in addressing some of the design and quality issues that have arisen on the lead ships—LCS 1 and LCS 2. We have previously reported that both ships had outstanding technical issues at the time of delivery, and the Navy has continued to discover additional problems.[8] For example, 17 cracks were identified on LCS 1 following delivery and after a period of operations; these had been predicted to occur by Navy and contractor structural analyses. Of these 17 cracks, 16 were in the topside, or deckhouse structure, and one was found in the hull. LCS 1 also has had issues with the failure of one of its gas turbine engines, corrosion, and a leaking seal on the propulsion shaft. LCS 2, which has spent much less time operating and has traveled fewer miles than LCS 1, has not reported as many major problems, but the ship has had corrosion in its waterjet propulsion systems that has required additional money to correct.

---

[8]Additional problems include the recent reports of a fire occurring on LCS 4 during the shipbuilder's initial sea trials and issues with water in the lube oil system on LCS 1. See also GAO, *Navy's Ability to Overcome Challenges Facing the Littoral Combat Ship Will Determine Eventual Capabilities*, GAO-10-523 (Washington, D.C.: Aug. 31, 2010).

According to the Navy and both shipbuilders, a number of design changes have been implemented on the lead ships and the follow-on ships of each variant to address and correct some of these problems. The Navy repaired the cracks on LCS 1 and implemented design changes (reinforcing weak areas) on LCS 3 and follow-on ships in the *Freedom* class to prevent the stresses that led to cracking. The Navy has also made changes to the configuration of several major ship systems, including structure, propulsion, communications, electrical, and navigation systems, to correct other problems. To reduce corrosion on both variants, the Navy expanded the corrosion protection system on the *Freedom*-class variant and added new corrosion protection systems to the waterjet propulsion systems of the *Independence*-class variant. The Navy also made design changes to the mission module bay at the stern of the Freedom variant to reduce corrosion and water build-up in that space. In some instances, the Navy paid for these changes, while the contractor paid in other instances.

Figure 2 identifies several of the significant design changes made to follow-on ships of each variant as compared to prior ships.

Figure 2: Major Design Changes among Littoral Combat Ship (LCS) Seaframes

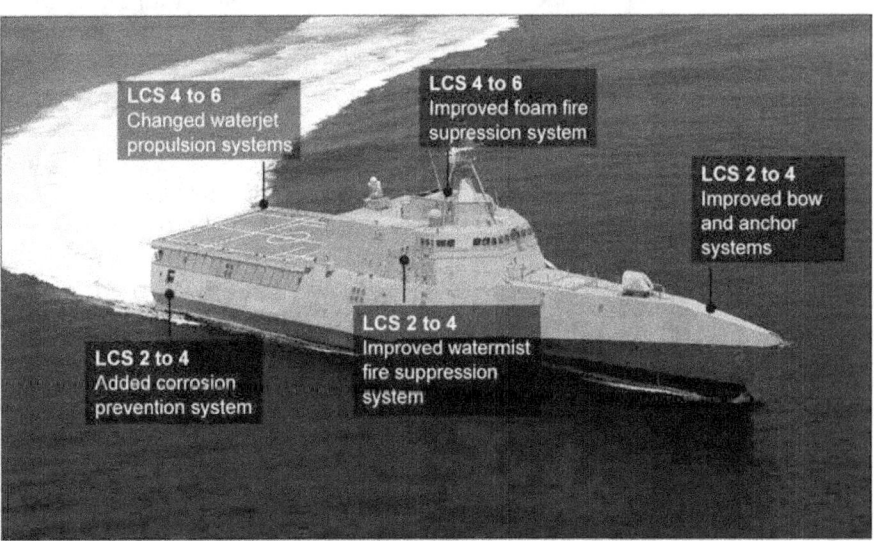

Source: GAO analysis of Navy data; U.S. Navy (image).

Freedom variant

Source: GAO analysis of Navy data; U.S. Navy (image).

Independence variant

The Navy and the shipyards told us that they have also taken steps to address weight growth, particularly on LCS 1, but seaframe weight remains a top technical risk for the program. Weight affects the speed and stability of the ship, as well as how much it can carry. According to Navy officials, LCS 1 experienced weight growth because the Navy directed design changes after the initial ship design phases were complete; the shipbuilder also underestimated the weight of paint and installed parts. As a result, the Navy had to use some of the weight margin allocated for future growth in order for the ship to meet the minimum requirements for mission package carrying capacity. Program officials also said that they had to implement design changes on LCS 1 and follow-on *Freedom*-variant ships to improve stability when damaged. On LCS 1, the Navy added two external ballast tanks to the stern following construction. For LCS 3 and subsequent *Freedom*-variant seaframes, the Navy designed these tanks into the hull, which adds 9 feet of length to the ship. This design change also provides added benefits of additional internal volume for cargo and fuel, which increases the range of this variant. While LCS 2 has also had issues with weight control, they have not been as significant as those on LCS 1.

Program officials and shipyard representatives for both seaframes said that they are actively managing the weight of the variants. Representatives from both shipyards told us that they monitor seaframe weight through a weight management plan, and all major design changes now require an estimate of weight impacts. In addition, the Navy said that weight control managers at each shipyard are responsible for weighing equipment over 50 pounds that goes on the ship. The Navy also told us that it has implemented design changes for lighter equipment and materials, such as a new electric start system for the gas turbines and gun fire control system. We requested updated copies of the contractually required weight reports that the shipyard is supposed to develop and provide to the Navy, but program officials told us these reports had been sent back to the shipyards to correct issues with the quality of the reported data that prevented these reports from being acceptable.

Cost, Production Efficiency, and Quality Have Started to Improve, but Schedule Delays Persist

LCS 1 and LCS 2, awarded under cost-reimbursable contracts, cost significantly more than expected, which is often the case for lead ships of a new class.[9] The Navy awarded fixed-price contracts for the 2010 block-buy contracts. As part of contract negotiations, the shipyards submitted estimated costs that decrease on each successive seaframe, with the expectation that affordability would improve on subsequent seaframes.

The Navy attributes these cost improvements not only to the use of fixed-price contracts, but also to the shipyards' experience building the ships. Both shipyards have worked toward improving production processes through the use of more automation and modularized assembly, as well as by increasing the amount of equipment and hardware that they install before the different large sections, or blocks, of the ship are assembled— a process called pre-outfitting. By increasing the level of pre-outfitting on follow-on ships and decreasing labor hours spent building the ships, production efficiency is gained. For example, both shipyards anticipate by the third ship of the class, they will achieve approximately a 50 percent reduction in the number of labor hours needed for ship completion.

Figure 3 depicts the actual and projected learning curves and pre-outfitting levels for both shipyards, where the data for LCS 1, 2, and 3 are actual data and the rest are projections. As is shown, increasing pre-outfitting helps decrease labor hours.

---

[9]GAO, *Defense Acquisitions: Realistic Business Cases Needed to Execute Navy Shipbuilding Programs,* GAO-07-943T (Washington, D.C.: July 24, 2007). Section 125 of the National Defense Authorization Act for Fiscal Year 2008 set a unit procurement cost cap of $460 million per ship for all LCSs procured in fiscal year 2008 and beyond. Pub. L. No. 110-181. Implementation of the cost cap was deferred two years, to apply to all LCSs procured in fiscal year 2010 and beyond by section 122 of the Duncan Hunter National Defense Authorization Act for Fiscal Year 2009. Pub. L. No. 110-117. The cost cap was amended by section 121(c) and (d) of the National Defense Authorization Act for Fiscal Year 2010 to $480 million per ship. Pub. L. No. 111-84.

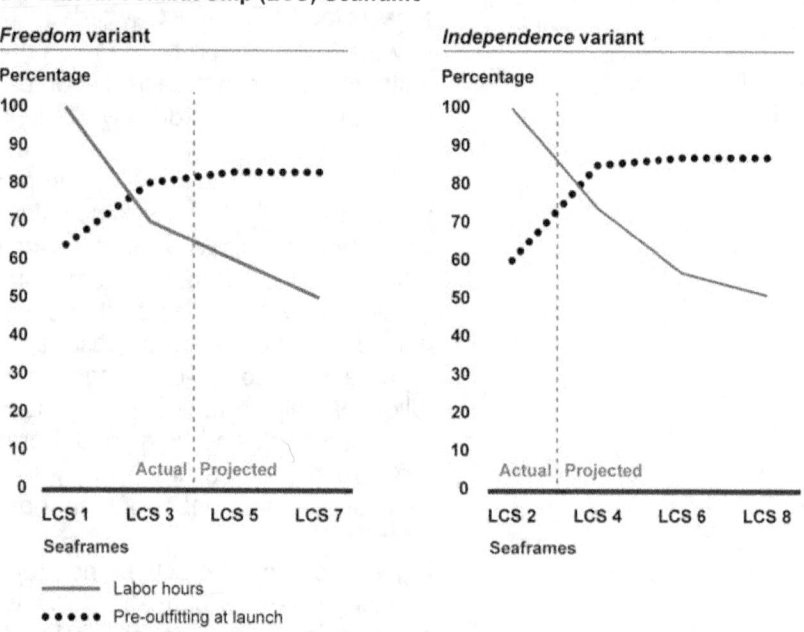

Figure 3: Actual and Projected Pre-outfitting and Labor Hours for Two Variants of the Littoral Combat Ship (LCS) Seaframe

Source: GAO analysis of Lockheed Martin (Freedom) and General Dynamics and Austal USA (Independence) data.

Note: Total hours are presented as a percentage with LCS 1 and 2 as the baseline.

The shipyards have also begun to realize the benefits of facility improvements. The fiscal year 2010 block-buy contracts provide for the shipyards to transition from building one LCS to a higher rate of production, which necessitated facility expansions at both shipyards. For example, Marinette Marine recently completed a 5-year, multi-million dollar investment program that improved its fabrication facilities, including its plate shop, panel line, and blast and paint facilities. According to shipyard representatives, they have also improved the flow of production through their facilities by eliminating 8 miles from their production sequence, which saves time in the movement of ship blocks that have to travel in the shipyard during construction. LCS 1 and LCS 3 were built in a more static fashion, LCS 5 and LCS 7 will represent the transition to the new production processes and buildings, and LCS 9 will be the first ship built entirely in the upgraded facilities. Austal USA also completed a multi-million dollar facilities expansion, including building a new module manufacturing facility. The yard also made production improvements, including expanding its use of extruded aluminum panels for the decks instead of welding individual sections, which Austal officials say could save significant labor hours per ship.

Navy program office and INSURV officials, as well as shipyard representatives, have described seaframe quality as improving. Deficiencies identified by INSURV vary in significance, and INSURV classifies these issues into three parts based upon the professional judgment of the inspectors. Part 1 deficiencies are intended to represent very significant deficiencies that are likely to cause the ship to be unseaworthy or substantially reduce the ability of the ship to carry out its assigned mission. Starred cards are a subset of Part 1 deficiencies that, in INSURV's view, require correction or a waiver by the Chief of Naval Operations before the ship is delivered to the Navy. Part 2 deficiencies are considered less significant issues that do not meet the criteria for a Part 1 deficiency, but should be corrected to restore the ship to required specifications. Part 3 deficiencies are generally categorized as those that prevent the ship from meeting Navy standards but are cost prohibitive to fix. Our analysis shows that the number of defects remaining at the time the ships were delivered to the Navy declined significantly from LCS 1 to LCS 3, but the number of seaframes delivered to date is too small to determine if this is a trend. LCS 2 has only had a partial acceptance trial, and LCS 4 has not yet conducted its acceptance trial (currently scheduled for June 2013), so the quality data on the *Independence* variant is limited and cannot yet be compared with follow-on seaframes. As of March 2013, both LCS 1 and LCS 2 each have seven outstanding starred cards that had not yet been resolved. Issues include the launch, handling, and recovery system on LCS 1 and the rescue boat and the way in which the engineering control system manages system trouble alarms on LCS 2.

Figure 4 shows the number of Part 1, 2, and 3 deficiencies and starred cards for each of the three delivered seaframes, showing a reduction in deficiencies between LCS 1 and LCS 3.

Figure 4: Number of Deficiencies Reported at Delivery for Early Littoral Combat Ship Seaframes

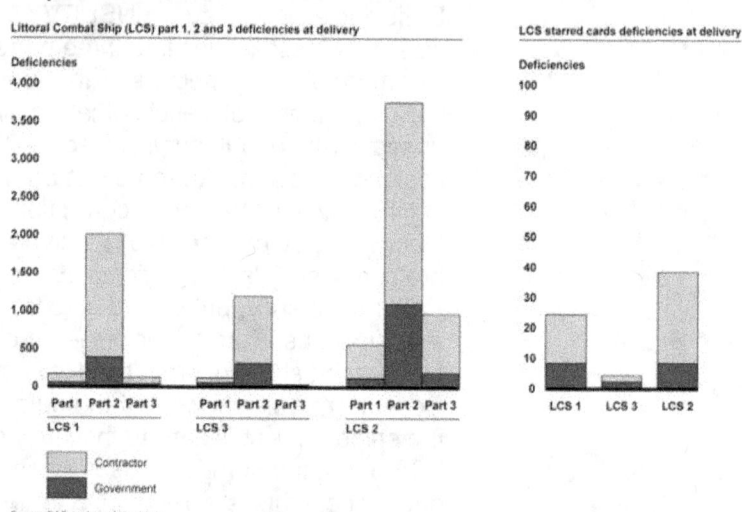

Source: GAO analysis of Navy data.

Notes: These data come from the Naval Sea Systems Command Technical Support Management system, and include all deficiencies open 7 days after the date of delivery. LCS 1 had a second acceptance trial after delivery, which resulted in additional starred card deficiencies.

Part 1 deficiencies are very significant deficiencies. Starred cards are a subset of Part 1 deficiencies that, in INSURV's view, require correction or a waiver by the Chief of Naval Operations before the ship is delivered to the Navy. Part 2 deficiencies are considered less significant, while Part 3 deficiencies are cost prohibitive to fix. Part 1, 2, and 3 deficiencies are also known as Priority 1, 2 and 3 deficiencies.

Deficiencies labeled as "Government" reflect those that were determined by the Navy and the shipbuilding contractor to be the Navy's responsibility for correction, while those labeled as "Contractor" reflect those that were determined to be the shipbuilding contractor's responsibility for correction.

One area of seaframe production that continues to be problematic is schedule performance for reasons related and unrelated to the LCS program. The lead ships were each delivered almost 2 years after their initial planned delivery dates due to various design and construction issues. LCS 3 delivered 2 months ahead of its contractually required date, but the next five ships are expected to deliver, on average, 7 months late. Representatives at Marinette Marine told us that LCS 5 and LCS 7 are both delayed due in part to a commercial ship that is behind schedule and blocking shipyard workflow. At Austal USA, LCS 4 has been delayed several times due to use of less-skilled labor and delays in obtaining production drawings. LCS 6 and LCS 8 are expected to be delayed due to the shipyard's transition to its new production line and the workers' relative inexperience with it. The Navy has adjusted its delivery schedule for future ships to take into account these delays and does not envision further delays beyond LCS 8.

Figure 5 shows the total construction time for LCS 1 through LCS 8 and their delivery delays.

Figure 5: Littoral Combat Ship (LCS) Construction Timeframes

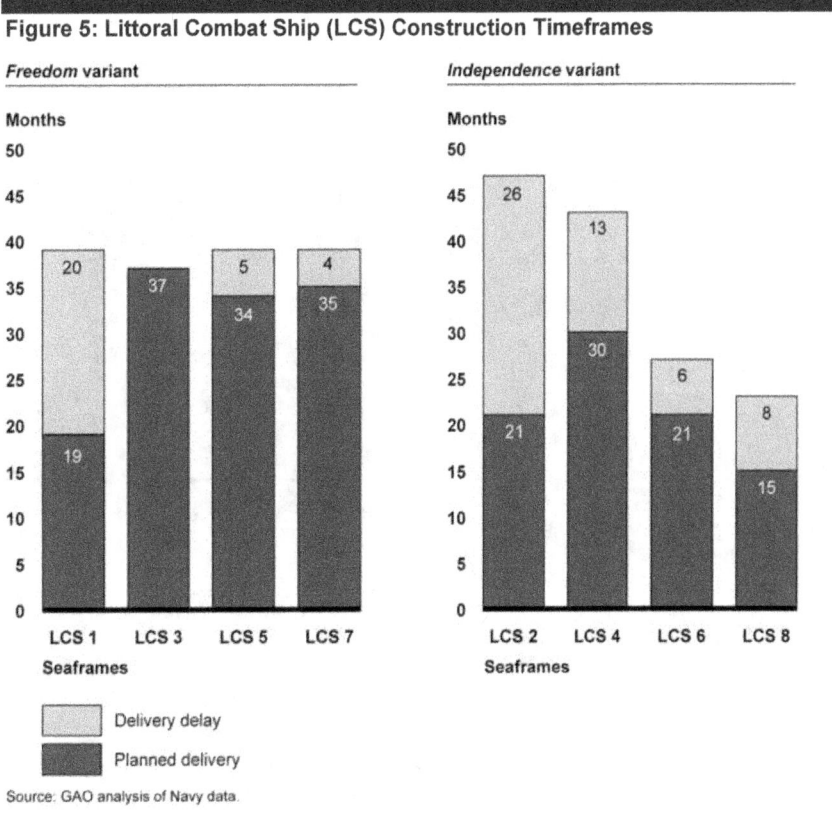

Source: GAO analysis of Navy data.

Note: Dates reflect keel laying to delivery.

Seaframe Designs Have Been Stabilizing, but Navy Is Considering Significant Changes

Even as production is underway at the two shipyards, the Navy is evaluating various options for changes to LCS seaframe designs. The program office has several studies ongoing to evaluate changes to the seaframes, communication networks, combat management systems, and hull, mechanical, and electrical systems. Shipyard experience, which translates into reduced labor hours expended per ship, is based on building repeat copies of similar ships, and design changes can disrupt this learning. To date, the number of design changes that the Navy is implementing on the two variants has been decreasing.

Figure 6 depicts the decrease in design changes on both variants.

Figure 6: Decrease in Littoral Combat Ship (LCS) Design Changes for Both Seaframe Variants

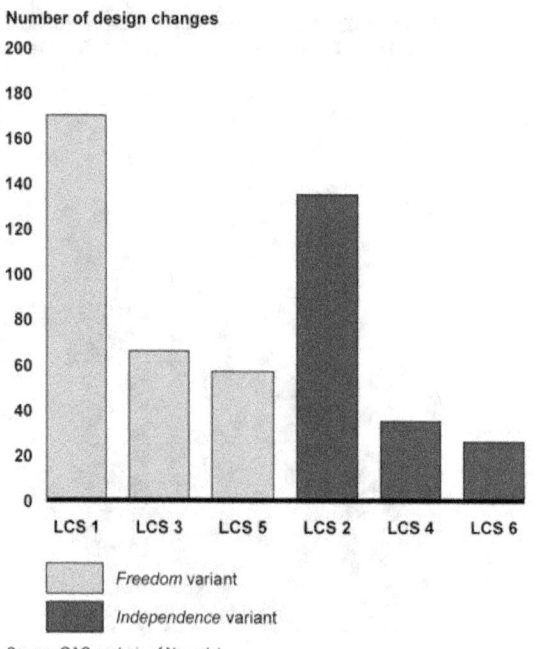

Source: GAO analysis of Navy data.

However, the Navy is now considering a series of potentially significant design changes to accommodate larger crews than initially anticipated, increase commonality between the seaframe variants and with other Navy ships, and increase the ships' combat capabilities, among others. For example, prior to the deployment of LCS 1 to Singapore, the Navy added 20 extra berths to the ship and intends to make a similar change to LCS 2. However, the Navy did not add equivalent amounts of crew storage space; the ships will also require additional water and sanitation systems and food storage to meet Navy standards. The Navy is now evaluating how to make these additional berths better suited to both variant designs. The Navy also has a number of technical studies underway that could affect design, including an OPNAV study on potential capability changes and a requirements analysis for a notional LCS Flight 1 seaframe, and a Naval Sea Systems Command Flight 1 technology assessment study. According to Navy program office officials, some of these changes could increase the acquisition cost of the seaframes due to disrupting shipyard learning and could also increase operations and support costs, due to factors such as additional crew. Other changes, such as moving to more common equipment among both variants, could reduce operations and support costs due to reducing the number of unique spare parts that have to be maintained and different training required for maintenance and training.

The design changes that the Navy is evaluating include the following:

- **Changes to increase commonality:** Many of the systems on the two seaframe variants are not common. Both contractors choose different ways of optimizing the cost and performance of the seaframes they proposed to the Navy. When the Navy chose to buy both variants, it committed to buying ships with differing equipment. Some systems are not common between the LCS variants, but are common with other ships in the fleet; others are not common with any other Navy ship. DOD's office of Cost Assessment and Program Evaluation stated in its 2011 independent cost estimate of LCS seaframes that if the Navy down-selected to one variant and sold or decommissioned the variant that was not selected, it could have saved approximately $2.2 billion in operations and support costs in fiscal year 2010 dollars. A lack of commonality may also hinder effective and efficient maintenance, training, manning, and logistics. One of the Navy's high priority changes is to select a common combat management system for both seaframes, since the different systems limit the ease with which sailors can operate each variant. The combat management system is an architecture that uses computers to integrate sensors (such as a radar) with shipboard weapon systems. INSURV identified 36 out of 52 major systems that should be made common between the two variants, and the Navy is currently evaluating the business case for each of these changes.

- **Changes to add capability and changes to requirements:** The Navy is assessing the possibility of increasing the combat capability of the seaframe by adding or enhancing onboard weapon systems and command, control, and intelligence systems, such as radar and satellite communications systems. The Navy is also assessing potentially changing some LCS requirements. For example, a senior LCS council official stated that the Navy is considering a potential reduction in the speed requirement for some seaframes. While this could require significant changes to the seaframe designs and therefore increase the program's acquisition cost, it might allow removing the gas turbines needed for high speeds, and thus could increase range and available payload space. Also, DOD directed the program office to develop an "irregular warfare" module, which includes medical and humanitarian relief supplies such as hospital beds and training facilities. Congress has not yet appropriated funding for this effort. The Navy is also considering additional mission modules for intelligence, surveillance, and reconnaissance and expeditionary warfare. The purpose of LCS's modular design is to help to ease the integration of new capabilities, but if additional power or cooling is needed or if changes are needed in the seaframe itself, design changes could be required.

- **Changes to LCS build specifications:** The Navy used American Bureau of Shipping rules to develop the functional designs of the LCS. In addition, the Navy has approved build specifications that are the variant specific contract requirements for detail design and construction. The Navy ended its relationship with the American Bureau of Shipping for surface combatants in June 2012, according to Navy officials, in order to save money. Ending this relationship should not on its own affect the build specifications for the ships currently under contract. Any requirements changes developed for a new Flight 1 LCS will require changes to the existing Navy-approved variant-specific build specifications. Representatives from both shipyards told us that changing the build specification during production could result in cost increases and a potential regression in learning while workers learned how to build to the new specifications.[10]

We have previously reported that incorporating design changes during construction may disrupt a shipyard's optimal construction sequence, requiring additional labor hours beyond current forecasts. In addition, when ship construction is initiated before a stable design is achieved, the risk of costly rework and out-of-sequence work increases.[11] Program officials told us they will evaluate the business case for each of the changes when deciding if and when to implement them. For some changes, the officials noted that potential reductions in operations and support costs could justify making them as soon as possible. Navy officials also emphasized that in other cases, it may make sense for the Navy to wait until its next contract for seaframes planned for fiscal year 2016 to avoid production disruptions during the current block buy.

---

[10]The American Bureau of Shipping is a ship classification society that provides independent technical assessments to ensure vessels are built to an established set of technical criteria.

[11]GAO, *Best Practices: High Levels of Knowledge at Key Points Differentiate Commercial Shipbuilding from Navy Shipbuilding*, GAO-09-322 (Washington, D.C.: May 13, 2009).

Testing Incomplete on Both Seaframe Variants

The Navy has not completed testing of either seaframe, and late discoveries of deficiencies could result in further design changes. Most notably, LCS 2 has not completed its acceptance trials or developmental and combat system testing, even though the Navy accepted delivery of the ship in 2009.[12] In addition, neither variant has completed developmental testing or undergone shock and survivability testing. In 2012, the Director, Operational Test and Evaluation (DOT&E) noted that limited testing on LCS 2 precluded his office from further assessing that variant's capabilities and any deficiencies. Operational testing and survivability testing are required by statute to be completed prior to a program proceeding into full rate production. Due to the unique designs of the two variants, the Navy still has outstanding gaps in its knowledge about how these designs will perform in certain conditions. Testing is required to resolve these gaps and to validate assumptions and models.

LCS 1 and LCS 2 followed an unusual trial and acceptance process because, according to the seaframe program office, they were funded as research, development, test, and evaluation ships that were intended for experimentation and the Navy wanted to get them fielded as soon as possible. LCS 1 had a special trial in lieu of a final contract trial. LCS 2 completed a partial acceptance trial in 2009, but it has not yet been presented for a second trial. Instead, it proceeded to an early 21-week post-shakedown availability, which typically occurs approximately a year after acceptance and is used to correct deficiencies and make needed improvements. The Navy plans to combine the second half of the LCS 2 acceptance trial and the final contract trial into one special trial in the summer of 2013. LCS 3 was funded with procurement money, and has followed a more traditional acceptance process, and it is expected that the follow-on seaframes will do the same.

The limited testing to date has revealed deficiencies with core ship systems on both variants, including performance problems with the 57-millimeter guns and the integrated capability of the combat systems. Testing has also revealed multiple single points of failure, meaning there are systems that lack redundancy, which could cause a system shutdown, on both LCS variants. This problem could become more pronounced in mission module testing. Most notably, the launch, handling, and recovery systems and hydraulic systems that are integral to

---

[12]Section 128(a) of the National Defense Authorization Act for Fiscal Year 2013 directed GAO to review the Navy's compliance with federal regulations in accepting LCS 1 and 2. Pub. L. No. 112-239. We will issue a separate report addressing this mandate.

launching the mission module vehicles lack back-up systems, and the ships have limited available space to carry spare parts or tools.

The Navy discovered another significant problem during testing on LCS 1 that led to a design change. The aluminum ramp that is used to launch and recover vehicles from the ship started to deform when the crew left the SUW module's inflatable boat on the ramp during transit, contrary to procedure. This in turn compromised the door seal on the stern of the ship and allowed water to get into the waterborne mission area. The Navy had intended the boat to sit in a cradle next to the ramp while in transit so it could be rapidly deployed and to be lifted into place for launch with an overhead crane system. The crew however, found that this approach tripled the time it took to launch the boat, to approximately 20 minutes. The Navy directed that the ramp on LCS 1 be replaced with a steel version prior to its deployment.

The Navy still has knowledge gaps on several other aspects of seaframe performance because testing has been deferred or delayed. For example, the combat management system software on LCS 2 was delivered incomplete. The combat management system contractor stated that the system was delivered with less functionality than planned due to developmental challenges and the Navy's urgency to have the ship delivered. The combat system trials for LCS 4 will be the first time that the full capability of the system will be tested in a realistic environment, and the final combat management system software build and a hardware upgrade will not be available until LCS 6. When we visited LCS 2 in December 2012, the crew still had questions about the combat management system and radar because they had little operational experience with either, and because the weapon and sensor capabilities have not been integrated into the combat system. In addition, neither LCS 1 nor LCS 2 has gone through Combat System Ship Qualification Trials which can be part of operational testing. These tests represent an opportunity to verify and validate combat and weapon systems performance for new ships, and the Navy and test entities use data collected to issue warfare qualifications and certifications. Navy program officials believe that they have conducted testing that is at least as rigorous as Combat System Ship Qualification Trials during the developmental testing phase. DOT&E officials disagree, emphasizing that operational effectiveness and suitability can be assessed only through operational testing.

The Navy has also not yet conducted ship shock trials and total ship survivability trials. The Navy plans to conduct the total ship survivability trials in fiscal years 2014 and 2015 for the *Freedom* and *Independence* variants, respectively. The Navy delayed survivability tests from fiscal year 2011 to 2014 so that it could have time to complete damage scenario analysis. Shock trials for both variants have also been delayed by 1 year to fiscal year 2016, so they can be conducted with LCS 5 and LCS 6. The Navy considers these ships the most representative ships of each class for shock trial purposes because they include all the design changes from the early ships. DOT&E has reported concerns that the Navy deployed LCS 1 without completing shock qualification of many components, including gas turbines and switchboards.

Survivability testing is important because it can reveal equipment or system failures that may necessitate class-wide design changes. According to DOT&E, there are knowledge gaps related to LCS designs and structures, in particular the potential vulnerability of an aluminum ship structure to weapon-induced blast and fire damage. The Navy is planning to conduct surrogate tests with aluminum structures in fiscal years 2013 and 2014 to help address these knowledge gaps. LCS is built to a limited survivability standard, and, like material support ships, mine countermeasures ships, and patrol combatants, it is not expected to operate in the most severe or hostile environments. DOT&E has reported that the LCS is not expected to maintain mission capability after taking a significant hit in a hostile combat environment. Program officials state that LCS meets the survivability requirements to which the ship was designed.

Navy Acquisition of Mission Modules Is Risky Due to Inadequately Defined Early Increments and Continued Developmental Difficulties

The Navy's acquisition approach for mission modules is risky for three reasons: (1) the Navy continues to buy early increments of mission packages that lack defined requirements and clear definition of incremental cost, schedule, and performance goals; (2) developmental testing to date continues to identify problems with system performance; and (3) concerns persist about the overall effectiveness of each mission package. While the program is following an evolutionary acquisition strategy and plans to deliver improving levels of capability over several increments, the program continues to buy modules for mission packages without first documenting the level of performance that it expects for each increment. By the time the Navy demonstrates that it can meet the minimum—termed "threshold"—requirements identified in the LCS programs' capability development document in the final increments, it will have already bought 24 MCM and SUW mission packages.[13] Further,

[13]The Navy plans to meet the threshold performance levels defined in this document for the ASW mission package in the first and only increment of that package.

developmental testing to date—especially for the systems comprising the MCM mission package—has shown continued performance problems. Some of these systems do not meet their own performance requirements, which does not provide assurances that LCS-specific threshold requirements targets will be met when they are operated together in a mission package. Internal Navy studies and wargames have also raised concerns with the overall effectiveness of each package based on inherent seaframe or module limitations.

Navy Has Not Yet Fully Defined Early Increments

The Navy is pursuing an evolutionary acquisition strategy for the mission packages. This means that it plans to deliver improving levels of capability over several mission package increments. The Navy's threshold performance requirements as currently defined in LCS requirements documentation will be met only when the final increment of each package is completed, and not by each individual increment. DOD acquisition guidance permits this approach, stating that the objective is to balance needs and available capability with resources, and to put capability into the hands of the user quickly. It also states that the success of the strategy depends on consistent and continuous definition of requirements, and the maturation of technologies that provide increasing levels of capability. Some of the mission module systems are pre-existing programs that predate the LCS program by up to 10 years or more. Therefore, these systems have their own requirements documentation, including threshold levels that they are expected to meet. However, because the Navy has not defined LCS-specific requirements for each mission package increment, it is unknown how the requirements for these separate systems will contribute to the broader LCS capability once they are integrated into a mission module.

DOD's 2003 acquisition guidance, in place when the LCS program was initiated in 2004, did not require programs to establish separate threshold and objective values for each increment. Therefore, the LCS mission package requirements are not defined for each increment; the requirements documentation defines only the end-state threshold requirement (i.e., at the final increment) for each package. However, DOD's 2008 revision to its acquisition guidance added new requirements for programs that use an evolutionary acquisition approach.[14] Specifically, individual increments are now defined as providing a "militarily useful and

---

[14]Department of Defense Instruction 5000.02, Operation of the Defense Acquisition System (Dec. 8, 2008).

supportable operational capability." The guidance now requires each increment to have its own set of threshold and objective (known as "target") values set by the user. These values are important because they provide the parameters for future operational testing. In most cases, the military utility of a system is assessed based on its ability to meet the end user's threshold values for each key performance parameter that is set forth in its approved requirements documents. Although this new guidance was not in effect when the LCS program acquisition approach was approved, the revision indicates that DOD now expects programs to define threshold requirements for all increments.

The Navy program office believes that each mission package increment will provide more capability than the existing systems they are to replace. The program also expects that the capabilities of the MCM and SUW packages will improve significantly between increments I and IV, including in key metrics such as the clearance rates for certain mines, number of surface boat threats that can be negated, and the range at which the LCS will be able to engage these surface threats. However, DOT&E officials told us that they do not believe the Navy has adequate knowledge about how integrated mission module systems onboard an LCS will perform in an operational environment to be certain of this fact. Further, without documented requirements for each increment, there is no roadmap setting forth the path from the current, below-threshold level of capability to the expected threshold level for the final increments. Program and OPNAV officials have stated that the current plan is for each increment to have documented requirements in the form of capability production documents, to be approved by the Joint Requirements Oversight Council starting in mid calendar year 2013. Recognizing that the absence of documented requirements for the early increments poses a challenge for operational testers, OPNAV has drafted incremental performance clarification letters for Increment II SUW and Increment I MCM mission packages. These letters identify the requirements that the mission package should be tested against in initial operational testing. According to DOT&E officials, the Navy will have to update its test and evaluation master plan to incorporate phases of operational testing for all increments of mission package capability to be deployed for use in combat.

Both the 2003 and current DOD acquisition guidance state that each increment is to have an acquisition program baseline by Milestone B. This baseline establishes program goals—thresholds and objectives—for cost, schedule, and performance. The mission module program's Milestone B review is currently scheduled for late fiscal year 2013, though this date has already slipped several times. Program officials have stated that they do not intend to fully define the goals for each increment in the Milestone

B acquisition program baseline. In particular, they stated that they consider the entire mission modules program to be a single increment and as such, they believe that there can be only one cost estimate for the entire program, and not cost estimates for each mission package increment. USD AT&L officials told us that they returned a draft of the Navy's mission module acquisition program baseline for further revision because it did not provide enough detail about costs and schedules for each increment. It is important to note that the structure of the mission modules program complicates cost estimation. For example, the Navy's cost estimators told us the lack of a cost estimate for each increment is, in part, due to the difficulty of allocating the development cost of the modules to each increment. The structure of the program also makes it difficult to determine the full cost of fielding the LCS capability, since the program office incorporates some systems that were developed and funded by other Navy sponsors, and these development costs are reported separately by the other programs and not by the LCS program. Though this type of arrangement is not unique to the LCS program, 42 percent of systems in the LCS mission packages do not have their research, development, test, and evaluation costs included in the LCS mission modules estimate.

Challenges Persist in Mission Module Development

Developmental testing to date—especially for MCM mission package technologies—has shown continued performance problems which do not provide assurances that threshold requirements will be ultimately met in the final increment. These developmental challenges are notable given that the Navy believes many of these systems to already be mature, and some predate the LCS program. Further, these challenges are in developmental testing, not operational testing which is a more representative assessment of capability. In addition, continual schedule delays have resulted in the Navy not being able to field capabilities as quickly as planned. Specifically, the Navy has seen a delay in fielding Increment I of the SUW and MCM mission packages by 2 and 3 years, respectively, as compared to the test plans that it submitted in 2008.

Table 3 shows some of the delays in fielding mission module capability.

Table 3: Delays in Fielding Littoral Combat Ship Mission Package Increments

In fiscal years

Mission package	Increment I		Increment IV	
	2008 estimate	Current estimate	2008 estimate	Current estimate
Anti-Submarine Warfare[a]	N/A	N/A	N/A	2016
Mine Countermeasures	2011	2014	2013	2017
Surface Warfare	2011	2013[b]	2014	2019

Legend: N/A = not applicable.

Source: GAO analysis of 2008 Navy documentation.

[a]The Anti-Submarine Warfare package was restructured and the Navy now plans to field only one increment.

[b]The Navy deployed a SUW module to Singapore in 2013.

Mine Countermeasures Mission Package

The MCM mission package—intended to detect, classify, localize, and neutralize enemy sea mines while keeping the LCS and her sailors out of the mine field by using remotely operated vehicles—will not meet the threshold capability specified in the current LCS capability development document until Increment IV is fielded, currently planned for 2017. Further, most systems are behind schedule for initially planned fielding dates. The third increment of the package is planned to provide both minehunting, initially fielded with Increment I, and minesweeping capabilities. Minehunting is the process of using sensors to localize and identify individual mines for avoidance or later neutralization. Minesweeping uses either acoustic and magnetic emissions to detonate mines designed to target a ship's acoustic or magnetic signature (called influence mine sweeping) or a physical device to cut the tether of moored mines so that they float to the surface, where they can be detonated or recovered for intelligence purposes (called mechanical minesweeping). Navy mine warfare officials stated that minehunting is the preferred mode of clearing mines since it is more precise, but that minesweeping is sometimes the only option due to time or environmental constraints. While the Navy has taken delivery of three Increment I MCM packages and plans to receive one additional Increment I package in fiscal year 2013, very few of its capabilities have been effectively demonstrated to date. The modules in the package have experienced difficulties during development and significant shortfalls in performance, and two key systems have been cancelled due to safety concerns while deployed from a helicopter. In response, the Navy has taken a number of actions, as follows:

- It is exploring ways to improve the performance of module subsystems, implementing several pre-planned product improvement programs.

- It has reduced key performance requirements thresholds for average mine clearance rates for early increments from the requirements defined in the capability development document.

- It has modified operational tactics, such as requiring multiple searches to correlate results. The modified tactics address some performance problems, but add significantly more time to minehunting operations or cover less area.

- It has decided to delay the retirement of the mine countermeasures ships the LCS is to replace by 3 years due to expected delays in mission module deployment.

Figure 7, an interactive graphic, shows the planned systems and employment of the MCM mission package. See appendix III for the overview graphic from figure 7. The Navy states that the threshold capability defined in the capability development document will be met by Increment IV.

Figure 7: Navy's Progress Fielding Littoral Combat Ship (LCS) Mine Countermeasures Mission Package Systems

Interactive Graphic Click on "⊙" to see an overview the modules. Click "⊗" to close. For the printed version, please see appendix III.

⊙ Mine countermeasures mission package	FY14 Inc 1	FY15 Inc 2	FY17 Inc 3	FY19 Inc 4	Capabilities description	Est. fielding date 2010	Current
 Airborne Laser Mine Detection System	■				Detects, classifies, and localizes floating and near-surface moored mines in deep water.	2011	2014
 Airborne Mine Neutralization System	■		■		Identifies and neutralizes unburied bottom and moored sea mines in shallow water that are imprac ical or unsafe to counter using existing minesweeping systems.	2011	2014
 AN/AQS-20A Sonar	■				Provides identification of bottom mines in shallow water and detection, localization, and classification of bottom, close-tethered, and volume mines in deep water.	2011	2014
 Remote Minehunting System	■				Remote multi-mission vehicle (underwater) towing the AN/AQS-20A sonar used to detect, classify, locate, and identify minelike objects.	2015	2014
 Coastal Battlefield Reconnaissance and Analysis System		■			Provides intelligence preparation of the battlefield information, which accurately depicts tactical objectives, minefields, and obstacles in the surf zone, on the beach, and through he beach exit during amphibious and expeditionary operations.	2012	2015
 Organic Airborne and Surface InfluenceSweep System		Canceled			Provides organic, high-speed magne ic/acoustic Influence minesweeping capability where mine hunting is not feasible (adverse environmental conditions).	2012	
 Rapid Airborne Mine Clearance System		Canceled			Mounted 30-millimeter gun firing supercavitating projectiles to neutralize near-surface and floating moored mines	2017	
 Unmanned Surface Vehicle with Unmanned Surface Sweep System		■			Micro-turbine-powered magnetic towed cable and acoustical signal generator towed from an unmanned surface craft.	2015	2017
 Surface Mine Counter Measure Unmanned Undersea Vehicle (Knifefish)				■	Fully autonomous unmanned undersea system provides buried mine detection capability.	N/A	2019

■ Shows when a system is initially fielded.

Source: GAO analysis of Navy documentation (data and images).

Notes: FY = fiscal year.
Inc = Increment.

ᵃAirborne Mine Neutralization System will add near surface capability in Inc 3.

Four of the Increment I systems—the AN/AQS-20A sonar, the Remote Multi-Mission Vehicle (RMMV), the Airborne Laser Mine Detection System, and the Airborne Mine Neutralization System—being procured from different system contractors, have experienced difficulties during tests. Two of them face difficulties significant enough to warrant a change in planned operational tactics to compensate for poor performance. Operational testing will be required to fully assess these tactics, the systems, and the contributions that they make to the mission package.

- **AN/AQS-20A Sonar:** This sonar is the primary system for LCS minehunting, which is the process of using sensors to locate individual mines in the water column that will be neutralized at a later time or avoided. This is a pre-existing system, and the program is over 20 years old. During 2011 and 2012 developmental testing, this system experienced problems in achieving some of the threshold requirements defined in the system's own requirements documents. In particular, this testing showed that the system faces challenges with accurately determining the vertical location, or distance from surface, of the mine in the water. The system also detected a large number of false contacts exceeding Navy limits in two of three search modes, meaning that it falsely identified non-mine objects as mines. In order to mitigate these two deficiencies, the Navy has modified its mine warfare tactics. For example, LCS operators will now use a technique whereby the system re-examines specific contacts and collects additional data to help eliminate false contacts. This tactic is effective in improving performance, but takes considerably more time—in some cases taking twice as long—and correspondingly limits the platform clearance rate. The Navy is also funding a performance improvement effort to correct these deficiencies via hardware and software upgrades to the system. According to the system's contractor, these upgrades are the first redesign of the AN/AQS-20A sonars since 1994. According to the contractor, some of the 30 units that the Navy has already purchased out of a planned inventory of 94 will be backfit with these improvements.

- **Remote Multi-Mission Vehicle:** The RMMV is an unmanned semi-submersible vehicle that tows the AN/AQS-20A sonar (together they are called the Remote Minehunting System). RMMV testing has revealed reliability shortfalls over the past 5 years. While recent efforts have improved reliability, the system still falls short of what is required. Operational testing in 2008 demonstrated the RMMV had a mean time between failures (ability to function before an operational mission failure occurred) of only 7.9 hours, well short of its requirement of 75 hours. The Navy and system's contractor implemented a reliability growth plan in 2010, and system redesign efforts have improved performance. Follow-on RMMV testing demonstrated the system's mean time between failures has improved to 45 hours. The contractor and the Navy have continued to work on further performance improvements, but there is disagreement about their effectiveness. According to the contractor, mean time between failures improved to 64 hours during 509 hours of system testing concluded in November 2011. However, DOT&E officials reported that this improvement was predicated on limited test data collected in a minimally stressing operational environment. In addition, since the testing did not involve an RMMV integrated with the LCS, they believe it is difficult to draw any meaningful conclusions from these results. The most recent Navy developmental tests of an MCM module operated from an LCS were completed in December 2012. These vehicles experienced higher than predicted failure rates, requiring considerable corrective maintenance by support personnel. The Navy plans to begin procuring vehicles in 2017, but has already purchased 10 baseline units that will need to be backfit with improvements.

- **Airborne Laser Mine Detection System:** This is a laser-based system mounted on a helicopter that searches the water column to locate floating and near-surface mines. Test results have show that this system has significant problems with meeting some of the threshold requirements defined in its own requirements documents, including demonstrating the required ability to detect and classify mines at certain depths. The system also generates a high number of false positives, which require additional investigation. That is, it often incorrectly classifies non-mine objects, such as glints from the laser reflecting off the water surface, fish, or man-made objects (e.g., litter), as mines. As with the AN/AQS-20A sonar, the Navy is modifying its tactics to use multiple passes over the area to help correlate data and address these shortcomings, but while this tactic improves performance, Navy test reports identify that it also greatly increases the amount of time required to search for mines. The Navy is also funding additional system improvements to correct this deficiency. In November 2012, Navy testers reported that the system did not demonstrate the expected level of maturity and failed to meet several requirements, presenting a high risk to operational testing. In spite of its poor performance, the Navy has accepted delivery of 7 units and plans to procure an additional 15 units as part of a request for proposals due in July 2013.

- **Airborne Mine Neutralization System:** This is an underwater system that is deployed by a helicopter and controlled from the helicopter through a fiber optic cable; it moves underwater to target and destroy mines using onboard explosive neutralizers. Developmental testing has revealed problems with the system accurately locating mines; according to the contractor, this is due to the movement of both the water and the sensor, making it appear that the mines are also moving. The system contractor has developed new software to address this issue. Developmental testing also demonstrated problems with loading and unloading the system from the helicopter due to inadequate clearance under the launch and retrieval system. According to Navy test officials, if this situation is not corrected prior to operational testing, planned for fiscal year 2014, it may be a major deficiency impacting the MCM package's ability to meet search and clearance rates. According to the Navy, it has designed an alternative load and handling device for the Airborne Mine Neutralization System.

Technological and operational problems issues have led Navy officials to cancel other MCM systems and to make investments to replace the lost capability. For example, the Rapid Airborne Mine Clearance System—a cannon designed to destroy mines near the water's surface that was initially intended to be fielded in 2011—was cancelled due to performance problems. The Navy may replace this capability with a modified Airborne Mine Neutralization System by 2017. According to Navy and contractor officials, this system has performed well in preliminary testing. Additionally, DOD concerns with the safety of towing the Organic Airborne and Surface Influence Sweep system from the MH-60 helicopter led the Navy to defund this system, which was planned for Increment III. The Unmanned Surface Vehicle with Unmanned Surface Sweep System will replace this system in Increment III. The Navy also decided to no longer tow the AN/AQS-20A sonar from the MH-60 for the same safety reasons. Navy officials told us that they had not envisioned frequently using the sonar in this manner, so they said it should not have a major impact on capability.

Program office officials have stated that they believe the first increment LCS MCM mission package will not only be more effective than the existing mine countermeasures fleet, but that it will also, importantly, remove the sailors from dangerous minefields, as is currently required to perform the mission. However, the LCS uses a performance metric that is not used by the existing fleet, so comparing performance is difficult. Specifically, for the LCS the Navy measures performance through a "sustained area coverage rate" metric that evaluates performance based on the amount of mines identified and/or cleared from a set area of water within a certain time. While the Navy states that this metric more accurately reflects operational requirements, it is a new approach and is not how the legacy fleet measures performance so direct comparisons are difficult. Further, no Increment I module has yet been tested in an operational environment, so its expected performance has not been validated. Additionally, DOT&E and Navy officials told us that the model used to predict MCM performance has in the past contained optimistic or unrealistic assumptions.

The LCS will also lack any minesweeping capability until Increment III, which is a capability found in the current fleet. The existing mine countermeasures ships or allied ships may be needed to supplement the LCS if minesweeping is required before Increment III is fielded. Another difference from the legacy fleet is that LCS is planned to only deploy an influence sweep system. LCS does not currently have a requirement to employ a mechanical sweep system like that used by the existing mine countermeasures fleet. An influence sweep system will not detonate contact mines which are designed to detonate when they come into physical contact with a ship, so a mechanical system may be required in areas where contact mines are expected. Finally, the Navy notes that LCS will not have an "in-stride" capability—or an ability to find and neutralize mines at the same time—like the legacy fleet, since the LCS sensor data requires post-mission analysis before moving to the neutralization phase.

Surface Warfare Mission Package

The SUW mission package—intended to detect, track, and engage small boat threats; escort ships; and protect operating areas—will not meet the threshold capability defined in the LCS capability development document until 2019, when Increment IV is planned to be fielded. The Navy has taken delivery of four SUW mission packages, each including two 30-millimeter guns and 2 11-meter rigid-hulled inflatable boats that accommodate boarding teams. The program plans to introduce a surface-to-surface missile in Increment III and a more capable missile in Increment IV.

Figure 8, an interactive graphic, depicts the systems and employment of the SUW mission package. See appendix III for the overview graphic from figure 8.

Figure 8: Navy's Progress Fielding Littoral Combat Ship (LCS) Surface Warfare Mission Package Systems

Interactive Graphic Click on "⊙" to see an overview the package. Click "⊗" to close. For the printed version, please see appendix III.

⊙ Surface warfare mission package	FY14 Inc 1	FY14 Inc 2	FY15 Inc 3	FY19 Inc 4	Capabilities description	Est. fielding date 2010	Current
 MK 46 30-millimeter gun system	■				Two-axis stabilized chain gun hat can fire up to 250 rounds per minute employing a forward-looking infrared sensor, camera, and laser rangefinder.	2011	2014
 Maritime security module		■ª			Two teams and associated equipment on LCS that provide capability to conduct visit, board, search, and seizure operations against potential threat vessels.	2011	2014
 Surface-to-surface missile (Griffin Block IIB)			■		Modular 45 degree launch unit provides limited precision attack missile for use against moving and sta ionary targets.	2011	2015
 Surface-to-surface missile (Griffin replacement)				■	Modular vertical launch unit provides beyond line of sight precision attack missile for use against moving and sta ionary targets.	2015	2019

■ Shows when a system is initially fielded.

Source: GAO analysis of Navy documentation (data and images).

Notes: FY = fiscal year.

Inc = Increment.

ªPrototype version of the Maritime Security Module deployed on LCS 1.

Navy and DOD weapons testers identified a number of concerns with SUW systems based on testing conducted with the Increment II mission module on the *Freedom*-class variant in 2012. DOT&E identified reliability problems with the 30-millimeter gun and associated combat system that need to be addressed if the module is to achieve its desired level of performance. The Navy has established a review board to investigate any additional changes required to correct any deficiencies.

The Army's cancellation of its Non Line-of-Sight Launch System which had been planned for LCS means that the Navy may not be able to field a surface-to-surface missile as part of the SUW module that meets all the requirements of the SUW package until Increment IV. This missile was envisioned as critical to defeating surface threats at greater distances from the ship, and was cancelled in May 2010 due to technical problems, associated test failures, and rising costs. The Navy assessed over 50 potential missile replacements for LCS, and in January 2011 selected the Griffin IIB missile as an interim solution based, in part, on it costing half of the Non Line-of-Sight Launch System. The program now intends to purchase one unit with a total of eight Griffin IIB missiles, to be fielded in 2015, which leave other SUW module equipped ships with a limited ability to counter surface threats. However, Navy officials told us that they may reconsider this plan because of funding cuts related to sequestration. According to OPNAV, funding for Griffin development and testing has been suspended for the remainder of fiscal year 2013. OPNAV and the LCS program office, with LCS Council oversight, plan to investigate using a more cost-effective, government-owned, surface-to-surface missile system that would provide increased capability, including increased range. According to Navy program officials, the deployment of the Increment IV missile could also be delayed by over a year because funding reductions have delayed early engineering work and proposal development for the missile contract.

Anti-submarine Warfare Mission Package

The current ASW mission package is early in development, and is not intended to be fielded until 2016. The initial increment was delivered in 2008, but the Navy cancelled the increment after analysis showed the module did not contribute significantly to ASW capabilities. Based in part on that analysis, the Navy changed the requirements for the mission package to include a more effective and in-stride search capability (searching while moving) that could be used for deep water escort missions of high-value ships and submarines. The newly configured ASW mission package—still called Increment I and currently planned to be the only ASW increment—was designed to provide these capabilities using a completely different set of sensors and systems, and because it is designed to meet threshold requirements, will not require an incremental approach. The Navy highlights this ability to implement a shift in requirements as an example of the benefits of LCS's modular design, in that it allowed for an easy interchange of systems and modification of planned capabilities. The planned technologies—consisting of a variable depth sonar, multi-function towed sonar array, and towed torpedo defense capability—are considered mature, and some are already operational in other navies. It will be several years, however, before the technologies are integrated into the planned LCS configuration. According to the mission modules program office, the variable depth sonar performed well during early testing when it was being towed off a research vessel, and the Navy expects it to offer a high level of ASW capability.

Figure 9, an interactive graphic, depicts the current concept for the ASW mission package. See appendix III for the overview graphic from figure 9.

Figure 9: Navy's Progress Fielding Littoral Combat Ship (LCS) Anti-Submarine Warfare Mission Package Systems

Interactive Graphic   Click on "⊙" to see an overview the package. Click "⊗" to close. For the printed version, please see appendix III.

◯ Anti-submarine warfare mission package	FY16 Inc 1	Capabilities description	Est. fielding date 2010	Current
 Multi-Function Towed Array	■	Passive towed receive array with deployment/retrieval cable to detect acoustic energy.	Under development	2016
 Variable Depth Sonar	■	Active towed sonar with launch, handling and recovery equipment.	Under development	2016
 Light Weight Tow Torpedo Countermeasure	■	Towed decoys that emits signals to draw a torpedo away from its intended target.	Under development	2016

■ Shows when a system is initially fielded.

Source: GAO analysis of Navy documentation (data and images).

Notes: FY = fiscal year.
        Inc = Increment.

Questions Exist about the Effectiveness of LCS in Certain Warfighting Roles

Internal Navy reports sponsored by the Chief of Naval Operations and insights gleaned from Navy tabletop wargame exercises have raised several concerns about the limitations of the LCS mission modules. For example, the concept of employment for the MCM mission package currently does not include embarked explosive ordinance disposal teams that are used on the existing mine countermeasures fleet, though the Navy has told us that LCS could carry such personnel and that they are investigating how to integrate this capability. These personnel are able to not only render safe or to destroy mines, but can also exploit found mines for intelligence value, and OPNAV has identified their absence as a capability gap. In addition, Navy reports, wargames, and DOD Cost Assessment and Program Evaluation officials that evaluate the LCS program have identified classified concerns with the capability or planned capability and employment of the SUW, MCM, and ASW mission packages. Further, since LCS has only a self-defense anti-air warfare capability, it will require protection from a cruiser or destroyer in more advanced anti-air warfare environments, which reduces the LCS's ability to operate independently and occupies the time of more capable surface combatants that might be better employed elsewhere. For the ASW mission package, DOD Cost Assessment and Program Evaluation officials have raised concerns about the new ASW configuration's deep-water escort capabilities, stating that LCS is not designed to be survivable enough to stay and defend the escorted ship if potential adversaries attack. Further, OPNAV officials told us that with this new configuration the LCS will still be able to conduct littoral ASW, but that the water depths in which the LCS could operate may be limited because of the depths required to support deploying the towed arrays. Any changes to improve the capability of LCS in these areas could result in design changes and cost increases.

Significant Questions Remain Regarding the LCS Business Case As the Navy Commits to Producing More Ships and Modules

The Navy continues to buy LCS seaframes and modules even as significant questions remain about the program and its underlying business case. Elements of the LCS business case, including its cost, the time needed to develop and field the system, and its anticipated capabilities have degraded over time. There are also significant unknowns related to key LCS operations and support concepts that could affect the cost of the program and soundness of the business case. Finally, the Navy continues to pursue an acquisition strategy that is not aligned with acquisition milestones intended to ensure that sufficient knowledge is in place before resources are committed. By the time key tests of integrated LCS capability and survivability are completed in several years, the Navy will have procured or have under contract more than half of the planned number of seaframes.

Key Elements of the LCS Business Case Have Degraded, Remain Unproven, and Continue to Evolve

A business case is part of a knowledge-based approach to acquisition that, in its simplest form, is demonstrated evidence that the warfighter's needs are valid and that they can best be met with the chosen concept, and the chosen concept can be developed and produced within existing resources—that is, proven technologies, design knowledge, adequate funding, and adequate time to deliver the product when it is needed. Key elements of the business case on which the LCS program was predicated have degraded, remain unproven, and continue to evolve.[15]

Higher Than Expected Costs and Longer Than Expected Schedules

LCS has ended up being more costly and taking longer to field than initially planned. LCS was intended to be an affordable ship at $220 million per seaframe. But, due to cost growth and schedule delays on which we have previously reported, LCS will be more expensive than originally planned.[16] Congress increased the cost cap established for the program twice, first to $460 million and then to $480 million per ship.[17] The Navy also wanted to accelerate the process of moving from design to fielding of LCS as opposed to prior ships. In the 2004 LCS capability development document, the Navy expected an initial operational capability to be fielded in 2007, 3 years after program initiation. According to the Navy, the LCS achieved initial operational capability in 2013, 9 years after program initiation, with the deployment of LCS 1 to Singapore with an installed mission package.[18]

---

[15]We have previously reported on the soundness of the LCS business case. See GAO, *Defense Acquisitions: Realistic Businesses Cases Needed to Execute Navy Shipbuilding Programs*, GAO-07-943T (Washington, D.C.: July 24, 2007) and GAO, *Navy's Proposed Dual Award Acquisition Strategy for the Littoral Combat Ship Program*, GAO-11-249R (Washington, D.C.: Dec. 8, 2010).

[16]GAO, *Navy's Ability to Overcome Challenges Facing the Littoral Combat Ship Will Determine Eventual Capabilities*, GAO-10-523 (Washington, D.C.: Aug. 31, 2010).

[17]The National Defense Authorization Act for Fiscal Year 2006 set a cost cap of $220 million per ship for the fifth and sixth ships of the class, with adjustments for inflation. Pub. L. No. 109-163, § 124. The National Defense Authorization Act for Fiscal Year 2008 set a cost cap of $460 million per ship for all LCSs procured in fiscal year 2008 and beyond with no adjustments for inflation. Pub. L. No. 110-181, § 125. The National Defense Authorization Act for Fiscal Year 2010 further increased the cap to $480 million per ship. Pub. L. No. 111-84, § 121.

[18]In comparison, the time from program initiation to initial operational capability for the lead DDG 51 destroyer was approximately 12 years. The DDG 51 is a more complex ship than LCS.

Lower Expectations about the System's Capabilities

Navy expectations of LCS capability have weakened over time. We analyzed several iterations of validated LCS requirements documents on which the program was initially justified, as well as various system descriptions from program office documentation and several iterations of the two LCS CONOPS documents.[19] We found that descriptions of how capable LCS will be and how it will be operationally employed have changed over time. Expected capabilities have lessened from optimistic, early assumptions of high levels to more tempered and reserved assumptions in recent documentation. While more explicit examples of specific capabilities that changed are classified, table 4 depicts some of the more significant unclassified examples of the changes in Navy statements about LCS's capability from early in the program to today.

Table 4: Evolution of Navy Statements about Littoral Combat Ship (LCS) Capability

Concept	Early (2004-2008)	Current (2011-2012)
LCS's capability against adversaries	Primarily developed for use in major combat operations. Will gain initial entry and provide assured access—or ability to enter contested spaces—and be employable and sustainable throughout the battlespace regardless of anti-access or area-denial environments.	Current LCS weapon systems are under-performing and offer little chance of survival in a combat scenario. Not to be employed outside a benign, low-threat environment unless escorted by a multi-mission combatant providing credible anti-air, anti-surface, and anti-submarine protection.
How LCS will deploy	Will be a self-sufficient combatant designed to fight and win in shallow water and near-land environments without risking larger combatants in constricted areas.	Lacks the ability to operate independently in combat. Will have to be well protected by multi-mission combatants. Multiple LCSs will likely have to operate in a coordinated str ke attack group fashion for mutual support.

[19]Specific concepts of operations for LCS are articulated in a classified warfighting CONOPS that describes how the LCS will be employed as a weapon system, and in an unclassified "platform wholeness" CONOPS that describes how LCS will be operationally supported as well as manning and training issues. The Navy has written two iterations of the warfighting CONOPS (2007 and 2011).

Concept	Early (2004-2008)	Current (2011-2012)
How mission packages swaps will be utilized	Mission packages will be quickly swapped out in an expeditionary theater in a matter of days.	Mission packages can be swapped within 72 hours if all the equipment and personnel are in theater, which may take significantly longer. An LCS executing a package swap could be unavailable for between 12-29 days.

Source: GAO analysis of Navy documents.

Note: Documents reviewed include LCS capability development documents, LCS concept of operations, and LCS wargaming reports.

Key LCS Concepts Remain Unproven and Continue to Evolve

Our analysis of LCS documentation has also shown that there are a number of broad unknowns related to the LCS concepts that remain unproven and which, until resolved, will make it difficult to determine if the LCS business case is sound and whether the system can meet the warfighter needs within available resources. Several of the key concepts that underpin the program—such as employing modular weapon systems, highly reduced manning levels, and heavy reliance on off-ship maintenance and administrative support—represent innovative approaches that have not been used before by the Navy and have not yet been validated through operations. The Navy's 2011 warfighting CONOPS for LCS reflect these unknowns, stating in several places that the Navy will determine how to employ LCS only once it has gained operational experience. Navy Fleet Forces officials also told us that there is not yet any LCS-specific doctrine on how an LCS is to be operated. Similarly, the operational support-focused platform wholeness CONOPS state that annual updates are expected because LCS crewing, training, and support strategies are constantly evolving. Some of these questions, discussed in table 5, are likely to have impacts on the ongoing LCS acquisition, including what seaframe variant should be purchased and how the ships will actually be operated and supported.

Table 5: Major Littoral Combat Ship (LCS) Conceptual Questions Regarding Ship Operations and Seaframe Variants

Conceptual questions	Issue
Relative advantages of each seaframe design	Because the Navy changed its approach from what was to be a limited initial purchase of seaframes followed by experimentation to concurrent acquisition and experimentation, it is currently unknown if the unique design attributes of each seaframe make one or the other more suited to specific mission sets and/or theaters of operation. The Navy acknowledges that the two seaframes are different ship classes with distinct capabilities and limitations that will affect mission tasking and deployment. For example, the former Under Secretary of the Navy and others have posited that the *Freedom* variant may be better suited to the Middle East region and the SUW mission given its maneuverability, while the *Independence* variant may be better suited to the western Pacific region and the ASW and MCM missions given its longer range and larger helicopter deck. The Navy has not yet determined if it will down-select to one variant or contract for mission-specific variants.
Feasibility of the reduced manning	LCS is intended to operate with a crew that is one-fourth to one-fifth the size of other comparable-sized ships. LCS currently has a core crew of 40, plus 23 aviation detachment crew and 15-19 mission package crew. Internal Navy analysis has shown a concern with high levels of crew fatigue on the LCS due to the higher workload required to compensate for the fewer crew members. The LCS 1 core crew was increased to 50 for the Singapore deployment, and the Navy is considering permanently increasing the core crews to 50 or more to address crew fatigue and workload concerns. The mission module crews may also need to be increased as the Navy gains experience using all three modules.
Feasibility and mechanics for the novel shore-based contractor maintenance approach	The Navy is implementing a new maintenance concept for LCS, whereby it will heavily rely upon shore-based contractor and civilian personnel to support and maintain the LCS. The seaframe crew itself will conduct very little preventative maintenance; the Navy envisions doing this work pierside. This approach will result in more complex logistics than is usually required for forward deployed ships, since parts and personnel will have to be forward deployed. This approach is unproven; data gathered on the LCS 1 Singapore deployment will help the Navy to determine whether it will be feasible and cost-effective. If the Navy elects to have the crews conduct more preventative maintenance onboard, it may require additional crew and seaframe design changes to accommodate spare parts storage.
Mechanics of mission package swaps	The Navy has not yet determined where mission packages might be forward-staged and how frequently they may be swapped out. In addition to recent wargames demonstrating that these swaps may take longer than initially planned, there is still deliberation on what types of crew qualification testing may be necessary after a swap occurs. Additional qualification testing could in turn require more time to get the ship back out to sea.

Source: GAO analysis of Navy documentation.

Changes to any of the above concepts could affect the LCS program and employment of the ships. For example, if the Navy learns that one seaframe variant is more useful in certain mission sets or operating areas than the other, the Navy could down-select to a single design or change planned seaframe procurement quantities. While the Navy is currently buying both variants, Navy program officials, as well as the LCS Council chair, state that all options are under consideration for the next planned contract award in fiscal year 2016. Similarly, if the Navy determines that mission package swaps are no longer feasible, the ratio of mission packages to seaframes that the Navy plans on buying may need to be reconsidered. Finally, the LCS Council chair told us LCS performance requirements might change, with potential areas including reduction in required top speeds and increases in lethality.

Future Acquisition and Operations and Support Costs Are Uncertain

There is also still significant uncertainty related to the cost of acquiring, fielding, and operating the LCS because of unknowns about the future designs of the seaframes and mission modules, and the Navy's manning and maintenance strategy. While the current blocks of seaframes are being built under fixed price contracts, any major changes to the design and/or capabilities of future LCS seaframes and modules can result in additional research and development funding being required and increased procurement costs. A down-select decision—which the Navy has not yet ruled out—would also have implications on costs for both procurement and operations. Similarly, if the mission module program continues to add or remove systems the acquisition costs for the modules may also change. In addition, as with other major weapon systems programs, operating and support (O&S) costs represent the primary life-cycle cost driver for the LCS program. Table 6 depicts several areas of uncertainty that could affect LCS O&S costs.

Table 6: Potential Areas of Littoral Combat Ship (LCS) Operating and Support Cost Uncertainty

Reasons for cost uncertainty	Issue
Evolving support plans	DOD has not yet approved a revised version of the Navy's LCS Life Cycle Sustainment Plan. This plan is a summary of the LCS sustainment strategy being developed by the LCS seaframes program office, and it includes discussion about how the LCS will address issues including shore support; replenishment and refueling; maintenance; and training. Changes to any of these areas which the Navy states may be an outcome of experimentation could impact operating and support costs.
Evolving manning levels	The manpower concept for LCS is a departure from traditional Navy operations. For example, LCS will be the first ship to use such a degree of minimal manning, and one of the first surface combatants to use a rotational crew concept[a]. The Navy has not yet finalized the manning for the different LCS variants and mission packages, and assumptions are still changing. In advance of deployment of LCS 1 to Singapore the Navy added 20 berths to LCS 1 and 10 additional billets to the ship. Manning is the most significant life cycle cost driver for ships.

Reasons for cost uncertainty	Issue
Heavy reliance on contractor-based maintenance	Instead of having the ship's crew perform most preventative maintenance while underway like other ship classes, LCS will return to port periodically for contractor-led maintenance periods. The ship will be unable to conduct most forms of preventative and corrective maintenance at sea, including basic activities like corrosion removal and painting, and will not have many spare parts on board or crew tasked to conducting repairs. For the initial deployments, contractor maintenance personnel will be flown in from the United States. The Navy is operating under an Interim Support Plan contract for this work, but it plans to competitively award a longer-term contract that more fully reflects its support strategy in 2014. Until these contracts are negotiated and signed, the exact scope of work to be performed and the cost of performing it will be unknown. At the same time, the Navy is evaluating shifting some maintenance back to the ship's crew, which indicates that its strategy is still evolving. Adding crew to conduct maintenance would add to O&S costs, though costs may be offset by reducing reliance on contractors. Further, it is unknown how mission module sensors and systems will be maintained. Some of these systems are sealed units containing sensitive electronics, and the LCS is not envisioned to be equipped with electronics repair technicians or appropriate parts to conduct repairs. It may be that any damaged or malfunctioning systems will have to be removed from the ship and returned to the contractor in the U.S. for repair.

Source: GAO analysis of Navy documentation.

[a]Ballistic missile submarines, mine countermeasures ships, and coastal patrol craft also use rotational crewing.

At the Milestone B decision for the seaframe program, the Navy estimated O&S costs to account for 62 percent of the program's life-cycle cost estimate, or $87 billion of $124 billion in total ownership costs through fiscal year 2057.[20] The Navy's point estimate for the LCS seaframe program total life-cycle cost estimate was at the 10 percent confidence level, meaning that there is a 90 percent chance that the costs could be different—and likely higher based on the data—than the point estimate. The confidence level is an output of the statistical risk analysis of the parameters and assumptions used to build the point estimate. If Navy leadership chose a higher confidence level, the resulting estimate would have been higher. The uncertainty reflected by this estimate was largely driven by unknowns in O&S costs and a lack of actual data about how LCS will operate on which to base estimates. Over the years, we have reported that many programs overrun their budgets because original point estimates are unrealistic. While no specific confidence level is considered a best practice, we have reported that experts agree that program cost estimates should be budgeted to at least the 50 percent confidence level, but budgeting to a higher level (for example, 70 percent to 80 percent, or the mean) is now common practice.[21] The Navy believes

---

[20]In then-year dollars. The O&S estimate would be $50.4 billion in 2010 dollars.

[21]GAO, *Cost Estimating and Assessment Guide: Best Practices for Developing and Managing Capital Program Costs*, GAO-09-3SP (Washington, D.C.: Mar. 2, 2009).

that it was likely budgeted at higher than the 10 percent confidence level with DOD's 5-year future years defense program, but did not provide a percentage. Further, it stated that the majority of the estimate is outside of the future years defense program and has not been budgeted for yet.[22] The Navy's estimate for LCS total life cycle costs ranges from approximately $108 billion at a 0 percent confidence level up to approximately $170 billion at a 100 percent confidence level.[23]

As a result of the O&S unknowns, the Navy will not be able to more accurately estimate LCS O&S costs until after it obtains and analyzes operational data obtained over the course of several deployments of both variants and after it finalizes its LCS manning and maintenance strategies.[24] As data continues to be gathered and more seaframes are deployed the quality of the data will continue to improve. Though the Navy provided estimates for LCS-specific support concepts, it has little or prior experience with these concepts on which to build accurate estimates. Navy cost estimators told us that the initial LCS O&S estimates were derived from O&S costs for other Navy surface combatants like the Arleigh Burke class destroyers and the Oliver Hazard Perry class frigates which were then adjusted for LCS specific concepts such as crew size, maintenance and training and other O&S activities. However, they also told us that until some of these concepts are refined and actual data is obtained, it will be difficult to establish a more reliable estimate.

Production of Seaframes and Modules Is Proceeding without Key Knowledge about LCS Capabilities

The Navy plans to make significant investments in seaframes and mission modules before completing testing designed to demonstrate whether the integrated ship can perform its intended missions. In addition to awarding contracts for almost half of the entire planned number of seaframes ahead of testing results, the Navy plans to procure more than half of the SUW and MCM mission packages before it demonstrates they meet LCS's minimum performance requirements for their respective missions. Specifically, by 2010, the Navy had awarded contracts for 24 of the 52 planned seaframes, and it plans to award additional contracts in 2016, 3 years before it completes operational testing needed to prove the

---

[22]The future years defense program is DOD's 5-year investment plan.

[23]In then-year dollars.

[24]GAO, *Littoral Combat Ship: Actions Needed to Improve Operating Cost Estimates and Mitigate Risks in Implementing New Concepts,* GAO-10-257 (Washington, D.C.: Feb. 2, 2010).

performance of the integrated seaframes and fully capable mission modules.[25]

As discussed above, when the Navy awarded the contracts for the first 24 seaframes, neither of the two variants had completed developmental testing, and based on the current schedule, operational testing of the integrated capability (seaframes with mission packages) will not be completed until 3 years after the next planned contract award. The Navy does not expect to complete developmental testing for both variants until 2015, survivability testing until 2015, and full ship shock trials until 2016. Results of these tests could result in identification of design deficiencies, and the Navy will have limited time to act on this knowledge prior to awarding its next block buy contracts for seaframes, currently scheduled for fiscal year 2016. Further, the Navy expects to procure at least 31 of the 64 planned mission packages while concurrently conducting developmental and operational tests on LCS 2 and LCS 3. Operational testing is currently projected to be completed in 2019, 3 years after the Navy plans to award its next seaframe contracts. This testing will represent the first time that the capability of the seaframes—equipped with mission packages that meet the threshold requirements defined in the capability development document—will be fully demonstrated in an operational environment.

The LCS will execute its operational testing in phases. Each planned increment of capability for each mission package will be tested on both seaframes. Operational testing will be considered complete when the final increments of all the modules have been tested on each seaframe. Based on the current acquisition strategy, the Navy will have bought 24 seaframes, 9 SUW mission packages, and 7 MCM mission packages when the first phase of operational testing begins in fiscal year 2014. This approach puts the Navy at risk of acquiring a large number of seaframes with limited capability or having to retrofit a large number of systems if problems are discovered in testing. DOT&E has also noted that operational testing planned for fiscal year 2014 may not be successfully completed or may be delayed because of performance problems identified during developmental testing. Any delays to even these early operational test events will further limit the information the Navy has to support its ongoing acquisition decisions, and increases risks that the Navy will buy systems that cannot meet requirements.

---

[25]Not all of these seaframes have been funded.

Table 7 shows the Navy's planned seaframe contract activities and actual and planned purchases, mission package procurements, and operational test dates.

Table 7: Planned Seaframe Contract Activities, Mission Package Procurement, and Operational Testing of Mission Package Increments on Each Variant

	FY 2012	FY 2013	FY 2014	FY 2015	FY 2016	FY 2017	FY 2018	FY 2019	Planned total
Seaframe contract activities				Solicit proposals and source selection for second block buy	Second block buy contract award				
Cumulative seaframes funded[a]	12	16	20	24	26	28	30	33	**52**
Cumulative mission packages procured[b]	8	13	17	21	27	29	TBD	TBD	**64**
SUW	4	7	9	11	13	13	15	TBD	**24**
MCM	4	6	7	9	11	13	TBD	TBD	**24**
ASW	0	0	1	1	3	3	TBD	TBD	**16**
Freedom variant operational testing			SUW Inc I SUW Inc II		MCM Inc I MCM Inc II ASW	MCM Inc III	MCM Inc IV	SUW Inc III SUW Inc IV	
Independence variant operational testing				SUW Inc I SUW Inc II MCM Inc I	MCM Inc II MCM Inc III	MCM Inc IV ASW		SUW Inc III SUW Inc IV	

Legend: FY = fiscal year; SUW = surface warfare; MCM = mine countermeasures; ASW = anti-submarine warfare; INC = mission module increment; TBD = to be determined.

Source: GAO analysis of Navy documentation.

[a]Cumulative seaframes funded refers to seaframes for which the Navy has received or plans to have received the congressional appropriations. The 24 seaframes purchased, or planned to be purchased through fiscal year 2015 are under the previously awarded contracts.

[b]The Navy has not finalized the acquisition strategy for the mission modules after fiscal year 2017.

We have previously reported that this type of concurrent testing and production can lead to cost growth and schedule delays on acquisition programs. For example, we reported in 2012 that most of the Joint Strike

Fighter program's instability was the result of highly concurrent development, testing, and production activities.[26] We also reported that the Missile Defense Agency's decisions to move into production without verifying performance led to extensive retrofits, redesigns, delays, and cost increases.[27] The Navy's current acquisition strategy for LCS puts it at similar risk.

The LCS acquisition strategy has led to major acquisition decisions being made well before key DOD acquisition milestones that provide the framework for oversight. For example, Milestone B for Navy shipbuilding programs typically authorizes detailed design and construction for lead ships. For LCS, the Under Secretary of Defense for Acquisition, Technology and Logistics (USD AT&L) authorized the final system design at Milestone A, which typically marks the initiation of a shipbuilding program's technology development efforts, and Milestone B was not held until after the Navy had procured nearly half the planned number of seaframes. Figure 10 depicts the how the LCS program compares with the typical acquisition framework for shipbuilding programs.

[26]GAO, *Joint Strike Fighter: DOD Actions Needed to Further Enhance Restructuring and Address Affordability Risks*, GAO-12-437 (Washington, D.C.: June 14, 2012)

[27]GAO, *Missile Defense: Opportunity Exists to Strengthen Acquisitions by Reducing Concurrency*, GAO-12-486 (Washington, D.C.: Apr. 20, 2012)

Figure 10: Acquisition Frameworks for Typical Shipbuilding Programs and Littoral Combat Ship

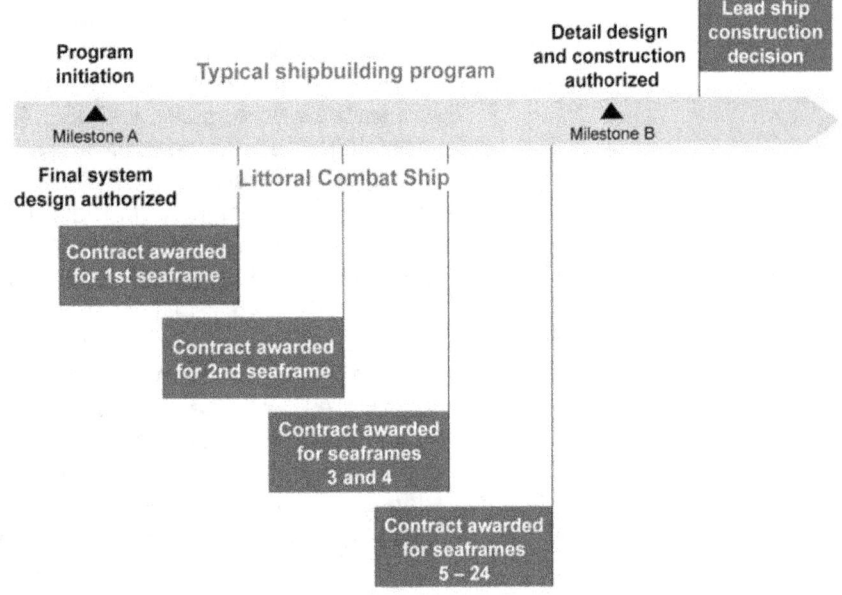

Source: GAO analysis of Navy data.

More recently, USD AT&L rescinded the requirement for the seaframe program to have a Milestone C review, and also delayed the full-rate production decision for seaframes from 2015 to 2019 because the Navy will not be able to meet statutory criteria dependent on the completion of operational testing until then. Statutes require the Secretary of Defense to provide that a program complete realistic survivability testing and initial operational testing before proceeding beyond low-rate initial production.[28] Statute defines low rate initial production for naval vessel programs, such as the LCS seaframe program, as production of the minimum quantity that is feasible while preserving mobilization of the production base. For the LCS seaframes program, USD AT&L has defined low-rate initial production as the first 24 seaframes. Unless the Navy changes its plans, its intention to award contracts for seaframes 25 and beyond in 2016 will exceed the low-rate initial production quantity 3 years prior to the full-rate production decision and prior to the completion of operational testing. While DOD acquisition policy does allow for decision authorities to tailor

[28]10 U.S.C. §§ 2399, 2366.

GAO-13-530 Littoral Combat Ship

information requirements and the acquisition process to achieve cost, schedule, and performance goals, the Navy's acquisition decisions on the LCS program are significant because each DOD acquisition milestone has associated criteria that are supposed to act as internal controls to prevent the premature commitment of resources before certain knowledge has been attained. The timing of this next planned seaframe contract award has also led USD AT&L and DOT&E to question the meaningfulness of the seaframe's full-rate production decision. Even though the milestone decision has been delayed, the Navy plans to continue purchasing seaframes, and if current plans come to fruition the Navy will have over half the planned seaframes under contract in the program's low-rate initial production phase.

The Navy has also made procurement decisions and committed resources to mission module production well in advance of acquisition milestones, essentially bypassing two major reviews. The Navy has procured 8 of 64 planned mission packages before Milestone B, which is when programs are typically authorized to begin system design and demonstration efforts, or Milestone C, which is when programs are typically authorized to begin low-rate production.[29] Making procurement decisions prior to these milestones—in essence, while the mission module program is still in the pre-low rate production phase—increases program risk because oversight organizations will not have yet approved key documents, including the acquisition program baseline, requirements documents, and test and evaluation master plan required for Milestone B.[30] The Navy planned to hold Milestone B for the mission modules program in fiscal year 2011, but it has been delayed until at least the third or fourth quarter of fiscal year 2013 because USD AT&L has not yet approved the acquisition program baseline. USD AT&L has delayed the decision until the Navy produces stronger linkages between the mission modules and the seaframes program and establishes metrics for

---

[29]Low-rate initial production with respect to a new system that is a weapon systems is production of the system in the minimum quantity necessary—(1) to provide production-configured or representative articles for operational tests pursuant to section 2399 of title 10; (2) to establish an initial production base for the system; and (3) to permit an orderly increase in the production rate for the system sufficient to lead to full-rate production upon the successful completion of operational testing. 10 U.S.C. § 2400(b).

[30]The acquisition program baseline is an important document for program management that shall include sufficient parameters to describe the cost estimate, schedule, performance, supportability, and other relevant factors. The test and evaluation master plan descrbes planned developmental, operational, and live-fire testing; measures to evaluate the performance of the system during these test periods; an integrated test schedule; and the resources needed to accomplish the planned testing.

individual mission package increments. In the meantime, the Navy continues to procure additional mission packages. The mission modules program office stated that the program's milestone decision authority has approved production of mission packages in order to keep pace with production of seaframes. In 2012, USD AT&L delegated the responsibility of milestone decision authority for the mission modules program from his office to the Secretary of the Navy.

In order to enhance oversight of the LCS seaframes and mission modules procurements, the USD AT&L has established that the Defense Acquisition Board—the department's senior-level forum for advising USD AT&L on critical decisions concerning selected programs—will conduct annual in-process reviews of the integrated LCS programs beginning in December 2012 and to be held each September thereafter. There will also be a Defense Acquisition Board review to coincide with the release of the request for proposals for seaframes LCS 25 and beyond. Additionally, USD AT&L has established that the Navy shall provide metrics to monitor progress in quarterly reports. These oversight mechanisms should provide USD AT&L opportunities to make decisions about future LCS procurements, but the information will ultimately be limited by the amount of operational test data available at the time.

Conclusions

The current LCS program is not the program envisioned over a decade ago. Initial cost estimates have been significantly exceeded; the Navy has not been able to field the ship or its planned capabilities much more rapidly than prior programs, as planned; and the supporting business case continues to evolve—including key unknowns such as how the ship will be used and manned. Further, the Navy will not be able to demonstrate that the LCS can meet the threshold capabilities defined in its requirements documentation with mission packages integrated with the seaframes until 2019. Until the Navy has solidified its requirements and concepts for LCS, neither Congress nor the Navy can be certain that the LCS is the right system to meet the warfighters' needs. Much is still unknown under the new concept the Navy has set forth. The Navy has a great deal of learning to do about the ships, the integrated capability that they are intended to provide when equipped with the mission packages, and how the overall LCS concept will be implemented. The deficiencies identified in this report are not criticisms of progress in the sense that things should have gone smoother or faster. At issue, rather, is the misalignment of the program's progress with acquisition decisions, and with key decisions being made well before requisite knowledge is available.

The apparent disconnect between the LCS acquisition strategy and the needs of the end user suggests that a pause is needed. The Chief of Naval Operations, representing the end user (the fleet), has sponsored several technical studies that raise fundamental questions about whether the program, as envisioned, will meet the Navy's needs. The results of additional, ongoing studies which are expected to be completed over the course of the next year or so may result in changes to the program. And the chair of the vice admiral-level LCS Council has stated that all options are on the table for the future of the program. In the meantime, the acquisition of seaframes and mission packages continues, and the program office shows no signs of slowing its next planned set of seaframe contracts. This disconnect between requirements and acquisitions increases the risk that the Navy is not wisely spending its resources. The Navy's request for funding for 4 additional seaframes (numbers 17-20) in its fiscal year 2014 budget request suggests that taxpayer money will be committed to 24 seaframes before important information is known about how the ship will be used. Congress is in a position to slow funding for these additional seaframes, pending the results of the technical studies that are already underway.

In addition, the Navy's approach of procuring the assets before the results of testing—which could potentially lead to design changes—is contrary to acquisition best practices. The work of assessing the results operational testing of seaframes, mission packages, and the integrated ship, as well as ensuring that cost estimates are well-informed and requirements validated, should not be rushed in an effort to adhere to the current schedule of awarding the next planned seaframe contract in fiscal year 2016. Doing so could lead to the Navy risking taxpayer investments of over $40 billion in 2010 dollars in systems that may not provide the expected—and yet to be fully defined—militarily useful capability.

Also, the Navy's planned approach of acquiring additional seaframes prior to a formal DOD full rate production decision limits the ability of oversight entities, including USD AT&L, DOT&E, and Congress, to be adequately informed and able to influence the Navy's actions. Equally important, if the Navy commits to a large quantity of additional seaframes before incorporating all of the lessons learned from fleet experimentation, it may end up buying equal quantities of both seaframes, when one variant may be in fact more suitable than the other. Likewise, the Navy's continued acquisition of mission packages that do not meet threshold requirements, and in the absence of a defined approach to meet these requirements in the future, is not in accordance with best practices or DOD guidance, and increases the risk that the Navy could buy a number of mission modules that are not militarily useful.

The Navy also still has a number of key decisions to make that could impact the design of the seaframes—such as increasing the level of manning onboard, adding additional combat capability, and moving towards ship system commonality—and that could significantly change cost estimates for the ship. The Navy may also learn via operational experience that each variant has better suitability to certain mission sets, which could influence the mix of future ships that it buys. This knowledge will likely not be attained until after several operational deployments with both seaframe variants employing all three mission packages. If the Navy signs contracts for another large block of ships in 2016 while these major questions remain, it increases the likelihood of continued design instability and production inefficiencies, as well as potentially fielding a reduced capability at a higher cost.

Matters for Congressional Consideration

1. To ensure that the Navy has adequate knowledge to support moving forward with future seaframe construction, Congress should consider restricting future funding to the program for construction of additional seaframes until the Navy:

   - completes the ongoing LCS technical and design studies,

   - determines the impacts of making any changes resulting from these studies on the cost and designs of future LCS seaframes, and

   - reports to Congress on cost-benefit analyses of changes to the seaframes to change requirements and/or capabilities and to improve commonality of systems, and the Navy's plan moving forward to improve commonality.

2. To ensure that information on the relative capabilities of each seaframe variant is communicated in a timely and complete manner, Congress should consider requiring DOD to report on the relative advantages of each variant in carrying out the three primary LCS missions. This report should be submitted to Congress prior to the planned full-rate production decision and the award of any additional seaframe contracts.

Recommendations for Executive Action

To ensure that, going forward, relevant oversight entities are able to provide appropriate decision-makers with additional insight into future contract awards for seaframes, we recommend that the Secretary of the Defense direct the Secretary of the Navy to take the following two actions:

1. If the Navy is approved by USD AT&L to award additional seaframe block buy contracts for LCS 25 and beyond, ensure that it only procures the minimum quantity and rate of ships required to preserve the mobilization of the production base until the successful completion of the full-rate production decision review. The award of any additional seaframe contracts should be informed by

   • a new independent cost estimate conducted by DOD's Cost Assessment and Program Evaluation office, and

   • a re-validated capabilities development document.

2. Prior to the full-rate production decision and the award of any additional seaframe contracts, report to Congress on the relative advantages of each seaframe variant for each of the three mission areas.

To facilitate mission module development and ensure that the Navy has adequate knowledge to support further module purchases, we recommend that the Secretary of the Defense direct the Secretary of the Navy to take the following two actions:

3. Ensure that the Acquisition Program Baseline submitted for the mission modules Milestone B establishes program goals—thresholds and objectives—for cost, schedule, and performance for each increment per current DOD acquisition policy.

4. To ensure that the purchase of mission modules do not outpace key milestones, buy only the minimum quantities of mission module systems required to support operational testing.

Agency Comments and Our Evaluation

We provided a draft of this report to DOD for review and comment. In its written comments, which are included in appendix II, DOD non-concurred with two recommendations, partially concurred with one, and concurred with one. We also provided relevant portions of the draft report to the shipbuilders and several contractors developing mission module technologies, and incorporated their technical comments as appropriate.

DOD non-concurred with the bulk of our first recommendation, pertaining to the quantity and rate of ships to be purchased under the contracts for LCS 25 and beyond. DOD stated that unnecessarily reducing production to a minimum sustaining rate would cause the price to the government to increase, with no value added to the program. While pricing of the individual seaframes is important, we believe there is greater risk in awarding additional seaframe contracts before key knowledge is gained about the LCS's integrated capabilities and how the ship will be operated. As we note in our report, when the Navy plans to award the next seaframe contracts, in fiscal year 2016, it will not have the benefit of this important knowledge, as operational testing is scheduled for completion in fiscal year 2019. DOD also stated that no major design changes are planned to the seaframes. But we found that there is, in fact, potential for such changes. As we note in our report, a number of ongoing technical and design studies, as well as the Navy's plans to move to a common combat management system and to increase the manning on the ships, are likely to require design changes. DOD agreed with the portion of our recommendation related to the need for an independent cost estimate to inform the planned 2019 full-rate production decision. Regarding the portion of the recommendation related to the need for a re-validation of the capabilities development document, DOD stated that the Joint Staff, along with the Navy, will conduct a requirements assessment study. It is not clear from DOD's response, however, whether this study will meet the intent of our recommendation, which is to ensure that the level of capability provided by LCS is militarily useful given the warfighter's current capability needs and that continued investment in the program is warranted. We continue to believe that a more formal revalidation of the capabilities development document, through the Joint Requirements Oversight Council, would achieve this goal.

DOD stated that it concurred with our second recommendation, regarding a report to Congress on the relative advantages of each seaframe variant for each of the three mission areas prior to the award of any additional seaframe contracts. However, DOD's response does not directly address our recommendation. DOD stated that the Navy can, if requested by Congress, provide a report on the performance of each seaframe variant and mission modules against current LCS requirements. While this may provide useful information, it would not address the relative advantages of the variants in performing the three primary LCS missions as we recommended. As noted in our report, Navy officials have stated that one variant may be better suited to certain missions or tasks than the other. We would expect DOD's report to Congress to contain this type of information to ensure that Congress is fully aware of the advantages and disadvantages of each seaframe variant and how these might influence future procurements. To help ensure that Congress is informed of the relative advantages of each variant prior to key upcoming decisions about future procurements, we added a second Matter for Congressional Consideration to this report.

DOD partially concurred with our third recommendation, regarding the establishment of cost, schedule, and performance goals for each mission module increment. DOD responded that the mission module program's Acquisition Program Baseline will include cost, schedule, and performance thresholds and objectives, but stated that the entire program consists of a single increment. This statement is inconsistent with how DOD defines performance requirements and how it plans to conduct operational testing for the mission modules program, both of which reflect individual increments. In addition, as discussed in our report, current DOD acquisition policy defines each increment of a capability, such as a weapon system, as a "militarily useful and supportable operational capability." Defining cost, schedule, and performance thresholds and objectives for each mission package increment would provide DOD and the Navy with information needed to effectively monitor the development of the increments and a baseline against which to measure performance.

DOD did not concur with our fourth recommendation, that the Navy buy only the minimum quantities of mission module systems required to support operational testing. DOD stated that the Navy must procure mission packages at a rate necessary to support (1) developmental and operational testing of the two seaframe variants with each mission module increment, (2) fleet training needs, and (3) operational LCS ships. The purpose of our recommendation is to facilitate mission module development and, at the same time, ensure that the Navy has adequate knowledge before it purchases additional modules to operationally deploy on LCS ships. Further, DOD's comments did not address the primary rationale for our recommendation—that the Navy is buying mission modules before it has met key acquisition policy and testing requirements and acquired the knowledge needed to validate that they work as intended. Instead, the pace of mission module procurements is based, in part, on the need to equip LCS ships currently under construction; that is, well before the ships would be available to be outfitted with module capabilities. As our recommendations point out, the way to mitigate the acquisition risks for the LCS program is not to maintain or speed up the current pace of procurements, but rather to adjust procurement plans to better align with the timing of operational test data availability.

The Navy also provided technical comments, which we incorporated as appropriate. The Navy also made three main points in these comments. First, the Navy stated that its experience in operating the LCS—over

100,000 nautical miles steamed on LCS 1 and 2 together—and conducting test events to date has provided enough information to give the Navy confidence that it understands the performance of the LCS and the program's potential risks. However, much of the experience the Navy has gained with LCS has been either with just a seaframe, or with partial or developmental versions of mission modules—not with complete, integrated, and capable mission packages. We do not believe that these activities are a substitute for or provide the same knowledge about LCS capabilities as operational testing. The Navy also disagreed with our characterization of the LCS business case as "degraded," stating that the program still meets the requirements defined in its capability development document. While this is true, several key assumptions about how the LCS would operate—that formed the initial business case—have changed. As we note in the report, the Navy's own internal assessments of LCS capabilities support this conclusion. Finally, the Navy stated that the initial increments of the mission packages are based on mature technologies and will provide a level of performance that exceeds the Navy's current capabilities and that subsequent increments will largely fill today's gaps in warfighting capability. As our report states, the Navy is still addressing development challenges with initial mission package increments, and their performance has not been validated in operational testing. The exact capabilities of subsequent increments is unclear because the Navy has not defined performance requirements for each increment or provided a roadmap for how they will meet LCS capability needs.

As agreed with your offices, unless you publicly announce the contents of this report earlier, we plan no further distribution until 3 days from the report date. At that time, we will send copies to appropriate congressional committees, and the Secretary of Defense and the Secretary of the Navy. In addition, the report is available at no charge on the GAO website at http://www.gao.gov.

If you or your staff have any questions about this report, please contact me at 202-512-4841 or mackinm@gao.gov. Contact points for our Offices of Congressional Relations and Public Affairs may be found on the last page of this report. GAO staff who made key contributions to this report are listed in appendix IV.

Michele Mackin
Director, Acquisition and Sourcing Management

Appendix I: Objectives, Scope, and Methodology

To assess the Navy's progress in producing and testing the seaframes, we analyzed Navy and contractor documentation including design reports and construction progress briefings that addressed performance. To identify design changes and to understand the impact of these changes to the construction processes for seaframes, we reviewed Littoral Combat Ship (LCS) contracts and change orders; master planning schedules for LCS 3 through LCS 8; Supervisor of Shipbuilding reports; reports to Congress; and Board of Inspection and Survey reports. We also reviewed information from contractors outlining process improvements and capital investments at each of the LCS shipyards aimed at increasing capability and capacity needed to support efficient construction of LCS seaframes. To evaluate testing and system suitability and survivability, we reviewed test reports and test progress briefings. Further, we conducted interviews with relevant Navy and industry officials responsible for managing the design and construction of LCS seaframes, such as the LCS seaframe program office; LCS Program Executive Office; Supervisor of Shipbuilding; American Bureau of Shipbuilding; Lockheed Martin, General Dynamics, and Austal USA (LCS prime contractors); and Marinette Marine and Austal USA (LCS shipbuilders). We also held discussions with LCS technical authorities, testing agents, and requirements officers from Naval Sea Systems Command; Board of Inspection and Survey; Director, Operational Test and Evaluation; and Commander, Navy Operational Test and Evaluation Force. We also met with officials from Cost Assessment and Program Evaluation, including the deputy directors. To observe some of the identified deficiencies and corrections on the LCS seaframes, we visited and toured LCS 1, LCS 2, and LCS 3. To understand how LCS was being integrated into the fleet, we met with officials from LCS Squadron One; Fleet Forces Command; and Third, Fourth, Fifth, and Seventh Fleets.

To assess the Navy's progress developing, producing, and testing the mission modules, we reviewed documents that outline LCS mission module plans and performance, including program schedules; LCS requirements documentation; classified mission module analyses; and recent test reports for surface warfare (SUW) and mine countermeasures (MCM) systems. We held discussions with Navy program offices; and with key contractors for the mission module systems that comprise Increment I of the MCM mission package and the contractor developing the Griffin missile, and saw examples of systems from these modules. We also met with officials from the office of the Director, Operational Test and Evaluation; Navy's Commander of Operational Test and Evaluation Force; Naval Undersea Warfare Center; Naval Surface Warfare Center; Naval Mine and Anti-Submarine Warfare Command; and Navy Space and Naval Warfare Systems Command.

To evaluate the Navy's business case for the LCS program and risks in
the Navy's acquisition strategy, we reviewed documents on the cost,
capabilities, and potential use of the LCS. This included documentation
related to LCS requirements, threats, and capability gaps, as well as the
LCS Warfighting and Platform Wholeness concept of operations. We also
analyzed warfighting and sustainment wargame reports; the Board of
Inspection and Survey's "LCS Material Condition and Maintainability"
report; and the office of the Chief of Naval Operations' "Review of the
Navy's Readiness to Receive, Employ and Deploy the LCS Class Vessel"
report. We reviewed LCS cost estimates, including the seaframes
independent cost estimate, and program lifecycle cost estimates for
seaframes and mission modules. To understand the level of unknowns
and potential changes with the program, we met with officials from the
LCS Council including the Director of Navy Staff, and reviewed the LCS
Program of Actions and Milestones document. To understand the
conceptual underpinnings of the LCS program, we met with officials from
the Naval War College and the Naval Warfare Development Command.
To understand the role of the fleet in defining the LCS concept and their
participation in the LCS wargames, we met with officials from LCS
Squadron One; Fleet Forces Command; and the officials from the Third,
Fourth, Fifth, and Seventh Fleets.

To assess the Navy's acquisition strategy for the integrated LCS program,
we reviewed LCS acquisition strategies from 2007, 2008 and 2010;
acquisition decision memos; program briefings; Navy reports to
Congress; acquisition program baselines; test and production schedules;
and contracts for both seaframe variants. We also reviewed relevant
sections of Title 10 of the U.S. Code and the Department of Defense's
acquisition policy for acquisition programs, and compared these
guidelines to the Navy's approach for acquiring the LCS. Additionally, we
interviewed officials from the Office of the Secretary of Defense, including
the Under Secretary of Defense for Acquisition, Technology and Logistics
and the Director, Operational Test and Evaluation; the Joint Staff; and the
Navy, including the seaframes and mission modules program offices; the
LCS resource sponsor in the Office of the Chief of Naval Operations; and
the Director of Navy Staff. Using this information, we identified how the
LCS acquisition strategy changed over time, and assessed how these
changes affected the alignment between the LCS programs' key test
events, such as initial operational test and evaluation; program reviews,
such as the full rate production decision; and investment decisions,
particularly contract awards. Finally, we leveraged previous GAO
reporting on the LCS dating back to 2005 to provide historical context for
these changes, and more recent GAO reports identifying challenges
resulting from concurrent testing and production activities.

We conducted this performance audit from April 2012 to July 2013 in
accordance with generally accepted government auditing standards.
Those standards require that we plan and perform the audit to obtain
sufficient, appropriate evidence to provide a reasonable basis for our
findings and conclusions based on our audit objectives. We believe that
the evidence obtained provides a reasonable basis for our findings and
conclusions based on our audit objectives.

Appendix II: Comments from the Department of Defense

THE UNDER SECRETARY OF DEFENSE
3010 DEFENSE PENTAGON
WASHINGTON, DC 20301-3010

JUL 1 0 2013

ACQUISITION,
TECHNOLOGY
AND LOGISTICS

Ms. Michele Mackin
Director
Acquisition and Sourcing Management
U.S. Government Accountability Office
441 G Street, N.W.
Washington, DC 20548

Dear Ms. Mackin:

This is the Department of Defense response to the Government Accountability Office (GAO) Draft Report, GA0-13-530, "NAVY SHIPBUILDING: Significant Investments in the Littoral Combat Ship Continue Amid Substantial Unknowns about Capabilities, Use, and Cost," dated May 28, 2013 (GAO Code 121050). The Department acknowledges receipt of the draft report.

As more fully explained in the enclosure, the Department non-concurs with recommendations 1 and 4. The Department concurs with recommendation 2. The Department partially concurs with recommendation 3.

The Department appreciates the opportunity to comment on the draft report. For further questions concerning this report, please contact Mr. Jack Evans, Deputy Director for Naval Warfare, at John.Evans@osd.mil or 703-614-3170.

Sincerely,

Frank Kendall

Enclosure:
As stated

**GAO DRAFT REPORT DATED MAY 28, 2013
GAO-13-530 (GAO CODE 121050)**

**"NAVY SHIPBUILDING: SIGNIFICANT INVESTMENTS IN
THE LITTORAL COMBAT SHIP CONTINUE AMID
SUBSTANTIAL UNKNOWNS ABOUT CAPABILITIES, USE,
AND COST"**

**DEPARTMENT OF DEFENSE COMMENTS
TO THE GAO RECOMMENDATIONS**

Navy Statement on the Littoral Combat Ship Program

The Littoral Combat Ship (LCS) program comprises two variants of seaframe and
multiple modular mission packages, each employing incremental fielding strategies. The
two seaframe designs (commonly referred to by the respective lead ship names,
FREEDOM and INDEPENDENCE) each meet the requirements established within the
program's Capability Development Document. Further, through innovative design
concepts introduced through the program's non-traditional acquisition strategy, the
performance characteristics of the two designs provide distinctly unique capabilities of
value to the fleet. Through the construction and lessons learned associated with the first
of class, each has achieved the degree of stability and maturity necessary to ensure
efficient production of follow ships. Perhaps most importantly, by virtue of sustaining
two production lines, the Navy has successfully employed competition in this program to
such extent that the unit cost in production is on a marked steady decline. At roughly
one-third the unit cost of our large surface combatant program, the competitive dual
sourcing strategy for LCS has provided the Navy with a viable approach to affordably
increasing our force while also addressing warfighting gaps.

The modular strategy for mission systems is a breakthrough concept for delivering cost
effective capability by employing mature technologies to meet today's warfighting
requirements while also providing tremendous flexibility to rapidly employ developing
technologies to counter emerging threats or otherwise close gaps today, and in the future.
The Navy has initially selected three mission modules for the LCS program: Mine
Countermeasures, Anti-Surface Warfare, and Anti-Submarine Warfare. In order to
deliver these capabilities in the capacity needed, and with an eye on controlling cost and
risk, the Navy is employing an incremental fielding strategy wherein the first increment
leverages mature technologies and existing programs of record to provide a level of
performance exceeding that available in the fleet today. Subsequent increments will
further augment this capability and capacity by introducing developing technologies and
systems which will largely fill gaps in today's warfighting capabilities. It is the Navy's
intent to deploy both FREEDOM and INDEPENDENCE variants with Increment 1
mission modules when each ship of the LCS program is ready to deploy. Later deploying
ships will be equipped with subsequent mission module increments as their respective
developing technologies are fielded.

Department of Defense Responses to Specific GAO Recommendations

RECOMMENDATION 1: To ensure that, going forward, relevant oversight entities are able to influence the acquisition strategy for future seaframe contract awards, GAO recommends that the Secretary of Defense direct the Secretary of the Navy to take the following action:

If the Navy is approved by USD AT&L to award additional seaframe block buy contracts for LCS 25 and beyond, ensure that it only procures the minimum quantity and rate of ships required to preserve the mobilization of the production base until the successful completion of the full-rate production decision review. The award of any additional seaframe contracts should be informed by:

    i.   A new independent cost estimate conducted by the OSD Cost Analysis and Program Evaluation office, and

    ii.   A re-validated capabilities definition document.

DoD RESPONSE: Non-Concur. The Department disagrees that the number of seaframes procured beginning with LCS 25 should be based solely on the minimum quantity and rate of ships required to preserve the mobilization of the production base until the successful completion of the full-rate production decision review. The Navy plans to procure LCS seaframes in accordance with the most recent long-range shipbuilding plan while balancing available funding with achieving the lowest possible pricing to the Government. Both LCS seaframe designs are stable and production processes at the two shipbuilders are being tuned to support the planned production rates. No major design changes are planned for either seaframe design beginning with the FY 2016 procurement, after the current block buys end in FY 2015. Unnecessarily reducing production to a minimum sustaining rate would only cause the price to the Government to increase with no value added to the program. The Department recognizes the unique situation of the LCS program relative to the defense acquisition system and is appropriately tailoring its decision-making milestones to suit. The Department will inform acquisition decisions with an up-to-date Service Cost Position and "should cost" assessment. The Defense Acquisition Executive will request a new OSD Cost Analysis and Program Evaluation Independent Cost Estimate to inform the decision. Additionally, the contract awards in FY 2016 will be informed by actual cost returns, not estimates, for eight delivered ships and an additional 16 ships under contract, but not delivered by FY 2016. The Defense Acquisition Executive will take into account the progress of the mission modules prior to approving additional LCS production. Finally, the Joint Staff, along with the Navy staff, will conduct a requirements assessment study which will serve as a revalidation of the LCS capabilities definition document. For reference purposes this recommendation will be identified as item GAO-13-530-01.

RECOMMENDATION 2: To ensure that, going forward, relevant oversight entities are able to influence the acquisition strategy for future seaframe contract awards, GAO recommends that the Secretary of Defense direct the Secretary of the Navy to take the following action:

2

Prior to the full-rate production decision and the award of any additional seaframe contracts, report to Congress on the relative advantages of each seaframe variant for each of the three mission areas.

DoD RESPONSE: Concur. Both seaframe variants are designed to meet the Capabilities Development Document specified requirements and support all three types of mission packages. Each variant is built to be compliant with the LCS Interface Control Document (ICD), which governs the interface between the ship and any current or future Mission Module. Future contract awards will be predicated on meeting seaframe requirements, including the requirement to embark any ICD compliant Mission Module, in the most cost-effective way. As the Navy prepares for the next procurement of ships, developmental and operational testing of the capabilities of each seaframe variant and associated mission modules is being conducted and the results will be used to inform future program decisions. The Defense Acquisition Board, chaired by USD(AT&L), will review the next seaframe procurement prior to Request for Proposal release. In conjunction with this process, the Navy can, if requested by Congress, provide a report on the performance of each seaframe variant and mission modules against the Capability Development Document (CDD) requirements. For reference purposes this recommendation will be identified as item GAO-13-530-02.

RECOMMENDATION 3: To facilitate mission module development and ensure that the Navy has adequate knowledge to support further module purchases, GAO recommends that the Secretary of Defense direct the Secretary of the Navy to take the following action:

Ensure that the Acquisition Program Baseline submitted for the mission modules Milestone B establishes program goals—thresholds and objectives—for cost, schedule, and performance for each increment as per DOD acquisition policy.

DoD RESPONSE: Partially Concur. The entire program, as defined by the Joint Requirements Oversight Council-approved LCS Flight 0+ CDD, consists of a single increment for the purposes of DoD 5000.02. The nine mission package "increments" (4 MCM, 4 SUW, 1 ASW) represent time-phased fielding of capability. The major systems that comprise mission packages are established as individual programs, with their own Acquisition Program Baselines (APBs) including cost, schedule, and performance objectives and thresholds. One APB for the entire mission modules program, which integrates these programs for LCS, is appropriate and compliant with law, regulation, and policy. The APB will include well-defined, quantitative cost, schedule, and performance thresholds and objectives for the mission modules. This is similar to the approach used for other programs which provide time-phased capability for platforms. The time-phased fielding of capability and the associated performance metrics to conduct testing against will be defined in the Capability Production Documents currently under development for each mission package. For reference purposes this recommendation will be identified as item GAO-13-530-03.

3

RECOMMENDATION 4: To facilitate mission module development and ensure that
the Navy has adequate knowledge to support further module purchases, GAO
recommends that the Secretary of the Defense direct the Secretary of the Navy to take the
following action:

To ensure that the mission modules do not outpace key milestones, buy only the
minimum quantities of mission module systems required to support operational testing.

DoD RESPONSE: Non-Concur. The Department agrees that LCS mission module
procurements should not outpace delivery of the LCS seaframes. To keep pace with the
LCS seaframes currently under contract or remaining under the current block buy through
FY 2015, the Navy must procure mission packages at a rate necessary to support:
1) developmental and initial operational test and evaluation of the two LCS variants;
2) developmental and operational testing of each incremental mission module capability
as it is integrated and fielded; 3) Fleet training needs; and 4) operational LCS units with
the tailored capabilities required for ship deployments. The Navy conducted a Quick
Reaction Assessment prior to the deployment of USS FREEDOM (LCS 1) and plans to
conduct Initial Operational Test and Evaluation of mission modules in ships, in
accordance with the approved CDD, prior to operational deployment of those
capabilities. For reference purposes this recommendation will be identified as item
GAO-13-530-04.

4

Appendix III: Mission Package Overview Illustrations from Interactive Figures

This appendix includes the overview graphics from interactive figure 7, figure 8, and figure 9.

Figure 11: Mine Countermeasures Package Overview

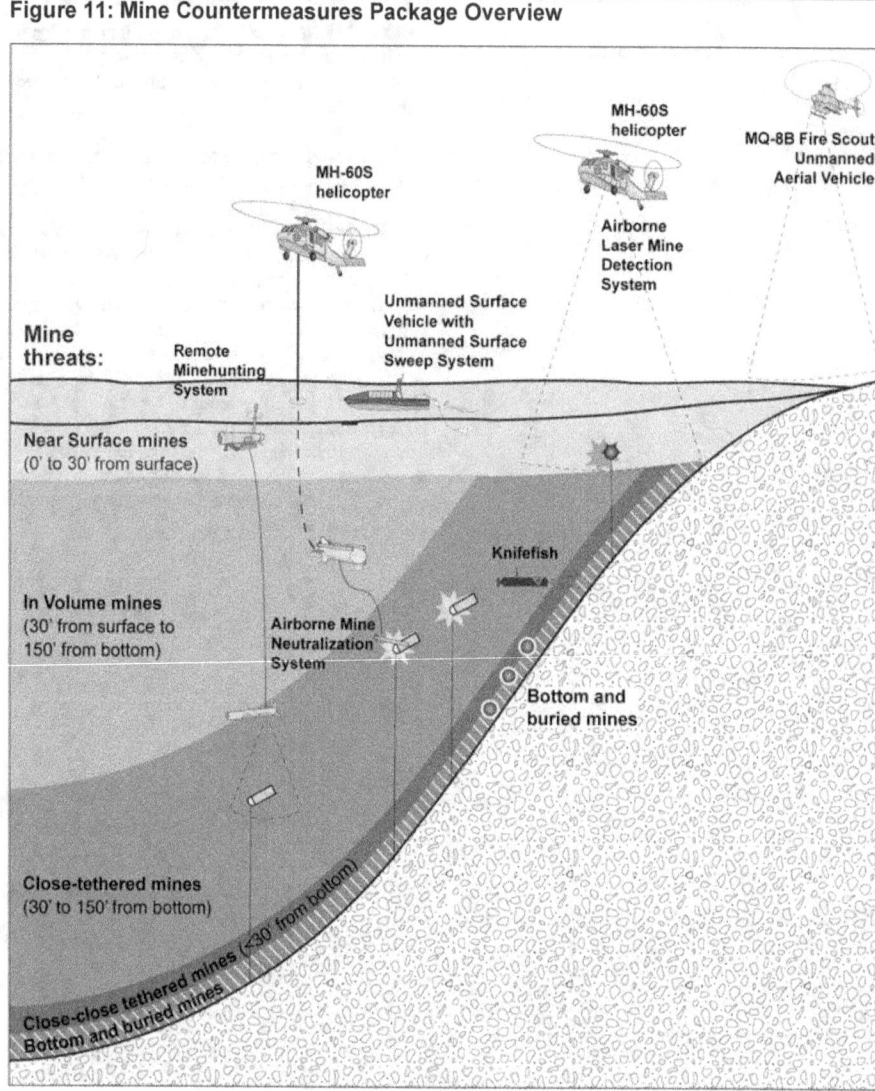

Source: GAO analysis of Navy data.

Note: Figure represents full capability, not Increment I.

Figure 12: Surface Warfare Package Overview

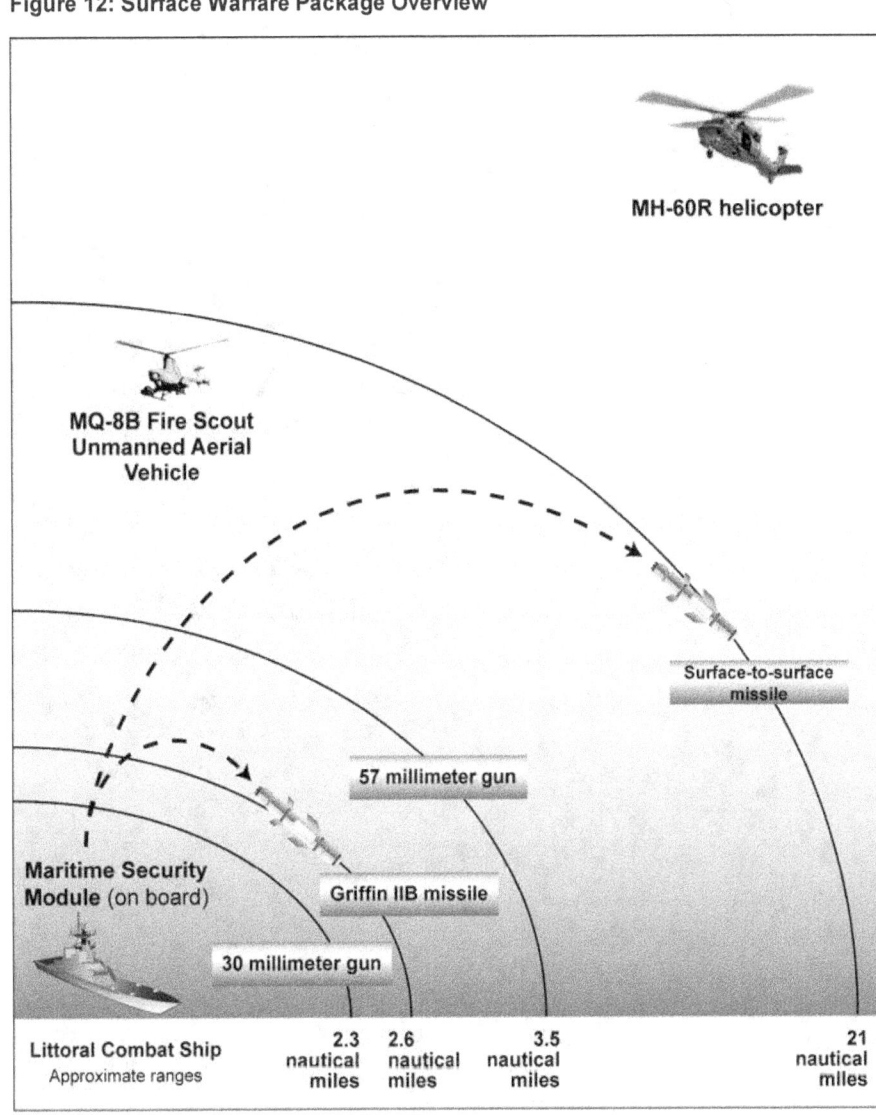

MH-60R helicopter

MQ-8B Fire Scout
Unmanned Aerial
Vehicle

Surface-to-surface
missile

57 millimeter gun

Maritime Security
Module (on board)

Griffin IIB missile

30 millimeter gun

Littoral Combat Ship	2.3 nautical miles	2.6 nautical miles	3.5 nautical miles	21 nautical miles
Approximate ranges				

Source: U.S. Navy.

Note: Figure represents full capability, not Increment I. However, Griffin IIB missile (or substitute) is an Increment III capability shown for illustration of its range only, and will not be in final package.

Figure 13: Anti-Submarine Warfare Package Overview

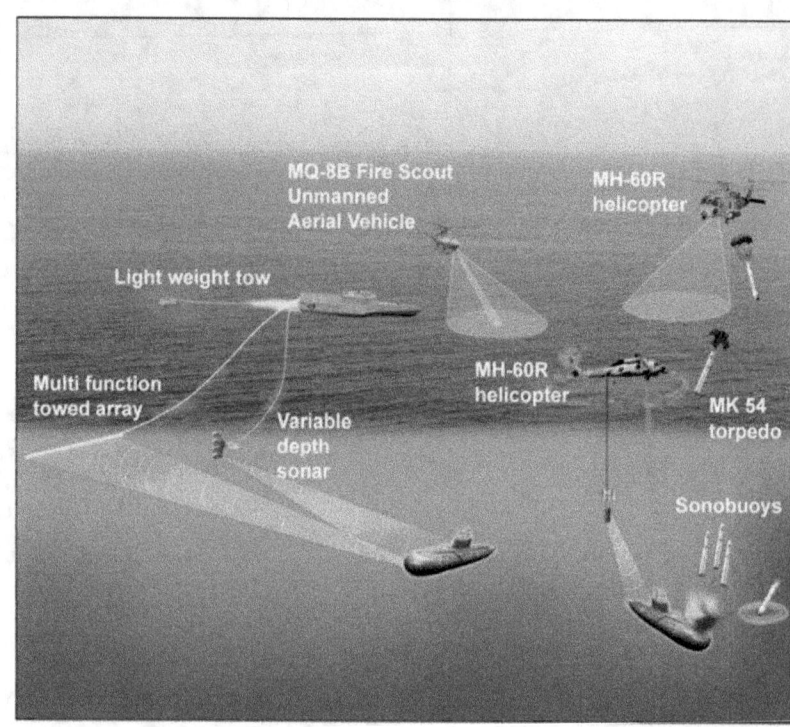

Source: U.S. Navy.

Appendix IV: GAO Contact and Staff Acknowledgments

GAO Contact

Michele Mackin, 202-512-4841 or mackinm@gao.gov

Staff Acknowledgments

In addition to the contact name above, the following staff members made key contributions to this report: Ron Schwenn (Assistant Director); Diana Moldafsky (Assistant Director); Jessica Drucker; Kristine Hassinger; Amber Keyser; C. James Madar; W. Kendal Roberts; Roxanna Sun; Robert Swierczek; Molly Traci; Hai Tran; and Nathan Tranquilli.

(121050)

GAO's Mission	The Government Accountability Office, the audit, evaluation, and investigative arm of Congress, exists to support Congress in meeting its constitutional responsibilities and to help improve the performance and accountability of the federal government for the American people. GAO examines the use of public funds; evaluates federal programs and policies; and provides analyses, recommendations, and other assistance to help Congress make informed oversight, policy, and funding decisions. GAO's commitment to good government is reflected in its core values of accountability, integrity, and reliability.
Obtaining Copies of GAO Reports and Testimony	The fastest and easiest way to obtain copies of GAO documents at no cost is through GAO's website (http://www.gao.gov). Each weekday afternoon, GAO posts on its website newly released reports, testimony, and correspondence. To have GAO e-mail you a list of newly posted products, go to http://www.gao.gov and select "E-mail Updates."
Order by Phone	The price of each GAO publication reflects GAO's actual cost of production and distribution and depends on the number of pages in the publication and whether the publication is printed in color or black and white. Pricing and ordering information is posted on GAO's website, http://www.gao.gov/ordering.htm. Place orders by calling (202) 512-6000, toll free (866) 801-7077, or TDD (202) 512-2537. Orders may be paid for using American Express, Discover Card, MasterCard, Visa, check, or money order. Call for additional information.
Connect with GAO	Connect with GAO on Facebook, Flickr, Twitter, and YouTube. Subscribe to our RSS Feeds or E-mail Updates. Listen to our Podcasts. Visit GAO on the web at www.gao.gov.
To Report Fraud, Waste, and Abuse in Federal Programs	Contact: Website: http://www.gao.gov/fraudnet/fraudnet.htm E-mail: fraudnet@gao.gov Automated answering system: (800) 424-5454 or (202) 512-7470
Congressional Relations	Katherine Siggerud, Managing Director, siggerudk@gao.gov, (202) 512-4400, U.S. Government Accountability Office, 441 G Street NW, Room 7125, Washington, DC 20548
Public Affairs	Chuck Young, Managing Director, youngc1@gao.gov, (202) 512-4800 U.S. Government Accountability Office, 441 G Street NW, Room 7149 Washington, DC 20548